R. GENE REYNOLDS

D1572008

Tyndale House
Publishers, Inc.
Wheaton, Illinois

to my wife Ruth
whose spiritual vital signs indicate
not only life,
but excellent health!

Scripture quotations are from
the *New American Standard Bible,*
© The Lockman Foundation 1960,
1962, 1963, 1968, 1971, 1972, 1973, 1975,
unless otherwise noted.
Quotations from *The New Testament: In
the Language of the People,* copyright 1937,
1965. Edith S. Williams, Moody Press,
Moody Bible Institute of Chicago.
Used by permission.

First printing, April 1982
Library of Congress Catalog Card Number 81-84599
ISBN 0-8423-0088-0, paper
Copyright © 1981 by R. Gene Reynolds
All rights reserved
Printed in the United States of America

CONTENTS

INTRODUCTION
5

ONE
I've Been There Myself
7

TWO
*Basing Assurance
on Just One Experience*
17

THREE
Trying to "Feel" Saved
29

FOUR
Learning the Vital Signs
43

FIVE
*A Life Style
of Willing Obedience*
51

SIX
The Holy Spirit Within Us
65

SEVEN
Loving Other Christians
75

EIGHT
Recognizing Our New Nature
85

NINE

*Confessing
Jesus Christ As Lord*

93

TEN

*The Last Step–
Confidence in God*

103

EPILOGUE

111

INTRODUCTION

If you are one of those countless thousands of evangelical Christians who cannot find satisfying peace about your personal salvation—this book is for you!

You do not have to live in a constant quandary about whether you have been born again. You can have "bedrock certainty" from the New Testament!

It may be that you have been approaching your assurance from the wrong direction. It seems that most doubters keep looking back to their "salvation experience" for assurance. The New Testament takes the opposite approach.

Allow me to escort you on a journey into assurance—an assurance that is more valid and permanent. If you have your "ups" and "downs" with assurance, surely it is appealing to discover that there is a certainty of salvation available to you that is constant, invariable, lasting.

I have had a threefold preparation which has equipped me for leading you on this journey.

First, I endured a period of doubting which lasted for many monstrous months when I was a young man. I attempted to find assurance in every way conceivable before I found it in Scripture. I think I can save you from several fruitless detours in your search.

Second, I gave special attention to this vitally important subject during the years of my academic study. Ultimately, I wrote a graduate thesis on John's doctrine of assurance, based on the Greek text of his first epistle.

Third, God has given me a "ministry of assurance." It has been a particular joy to me to walk with doubting Christians through their journey into assurance, and then see them blossom into maturity with the aid of their newly found certainty.

Let's take the journey together! We will investigate the "spiritual vital signs" as they give us an indication of our present spiritual condition. You will enjoy the travel. Our experiences are not identical. Mine were sometimes "pressure packed." At other times they were emotionally dramatic. At still other times they consisted of calm "reflections." Through it all, God was preparing me for this fulfilling ministry of assurance.

I am not attempting to force my experiences to fit yours, but through the journey together we will find that the great scriptural principles of the New Testament relate to *your* assurance just as they do to mine.

Gather yourselves up . . . . Let's begin the journey!

ONE
I'VE BEEN THERE MYSELF

We had talked for an hour. She had been doubting her salvation for several months. It seemed she would never have any peace about the matter. She had measured the time in resentment. Her physical features betrayed her inner despair.

As I watched the painful play of expression on her face, I thought a bit of humor would ease some of her tension.

I was wrong.

She blurted out, almost angrily, "It's fine for *you* to laugh! You're a pastor! You don't have the least idea what it means to wonder if you are saved!"

I responded easily and honestly, "Yes, I do. I've been there myself."

And I have.

I was born again as a youngster. Though the birth was genuine, I did not begin to grow immediately in my spiritual life. Through no one's fault but my own, my first ten years as a Christian produced little understanding of what the Lord wanted from my life. Like many child converts, I knew that when Christ saved me he had a claim on my life. But I thought of that claim in the most general of terms.

Through my years in public school I lived a decent life —I knew a Christian was supposed to live that way. But there was a spiritual void. Rather than allowing Christ to be Lord of my life specifically, I was committed to living a "Christian life" generally.

Upon graduating from high school, I entered Decatur Baptist College, in Texas, on a football and basketball scholarship. Athletics were my life—my only interest in college. I had been recommended to the coaches by a friend, Bill Tate, who was also there on a football scholarship. Bill was experiencing a period of stupendous growth in his spiritual life. He and another friend, David Kuykendall, introduced me to the New Testament concept of the "lordship of Jesus."

I thrilled to it! From the time of my spiritual birth, I knew Christ had a claim on me. But until those college days I did not grasp that he demands to be Lord of every facet of my life. It was a new, glorious day for me! The entire campus life nurtured my spiritual growth. For the first time, I *consciously* made Jesus Christ supreme Lord of my life.

As I began to reflect on my high school days, comparing them to my newly found commitment, I began to have some doubts about the validity of my salvation experience. At first, it was not the conversion encounter itself which I questioned, but the quality of life which followed. If I had been genuinely converted in the beginning, why did I not have the commitment to Christ during those first ten years that I had come to possess in college?

The thrust of every Christian testimony I had listened to had to do with the *experience* of being born again. This added to my doubts. With the weighty evidence of an evangelical background dominating my thinking, one thing I knew with great certainty: If I had not been born again as a youngster, I had never experienced the new birth.

By the end of the spring semester I was a very confused young man.

The events of the summer thrust a whole new world upon me. The Korean War was rampant, and I was conscripted for military service. Within a few short months I was assigned to Allied-occupied West Germany, in the famous resort city of Wiesbaden.

There was a dynamic group of American military personnel in Wiesbaden who conducted a weekly Youth for Christ meeting and led Bible studies on a regular basis. Both Americans and English-speaking Germans attended the Saturday night Youth for Christ rallies. We met in a large house at 14 Kaiser Wilhelm Strasse, one of the main thoroughfares of the quite picturesque city.

Because many German nationals attended the meetings, the emphasis was, wisely so, evangelistic. Our guest speakers for those Saturday night gatherings included American missionaries in Germany, servicemen who felt called to preach, military chaplains of an evangelical bent, and American evangelists making a "swing" through Europe.

Many of the Germans who came were not Christians; and many of them thought they could become Christians by "living a good life."

It seemed right, then, that most of the sermons were concerned with becoming a Christian, being saved, being born again.

I had not the slightest quarrel with the messages— their content or intent. Many of them did, however, add to my consternation about whether I had been born again. The nagging doubts from the college year had not only accompanied me to Germany—they had increased and were abounding!

My parents could have helped me, but pride kept me

from sharing my plight with them. It seems that most Christians who endure the spiritual stress of doubting their salvation find personal pride a problem. Most "doubting" is usually admitted only after one has worked through it.

I was only twenty years of age—a babe in the Scriptures as well as a too-long babe in Christ. John's first epistle was still an uncharted course; his teachings of assurance still alien to me.

Over a period of about eight weeks, three of our Saturday evening speakers employed the same logic to accent the need for conversion at a "point in time." The phrases utilized by the evangelists were identical almost to the syllable:

"If you do not know the *date* when you were born again, you have not been saved! You know the date you were married, don't you? If you don't know the date you were converted, you still need to be born again!"

I knew the motivation behind those remarks. Many of the listeners did not realize the need to be born again. The speakers were attempting to make them understand that one does not simply drift into the kingdom of God by living a good life—one must be *born* into it!

As good as it was for my non-Christian friends to hear, it was devastating to me in my own spiritual valley.

I was already suspicious of my "conversion" because early in my pilgrimage it had produced no obvious fruit. Now I had a new misgiving—I did not know the date of it! Though I was not married at the time I heard those illustrations, the speakers had well made their point with me.

If your own conversion experience has become suspect to you because of this kind of rationale, allow me to share two thoughts with you.

First, though some of us know the date of our marriage but not the date of our conversion, there *is* a difference. We *planned* to be married; we did not *plan* for the date of our conversion. Even among those who went through a "building up" to the day they received Christ, no one projected a spiritual birth on the planning calendar—"I'll get saved next Thursday!" Because I planned to be married and projected my life around the proposed date, it is indelibly cast in my consciousness: March 12, 1955. Such forethought was not a part of the days immediately prior to my conversion.

I could go to the church I attended as a boy and check the records; then I would know the *date* of my second birth. But I cannot recall it now. I did not consciously put it into my memory bank the day I was saved—though I do remember coming to Christ.

Second, dates mean little to youngsters, even to teenagers. Unless someone tells a youngster when he is saved to "mark down this date" he probably will not do it. Many people who were converted as adults do not know the date of their experience; it is even less likely that child converts would remember the exact calendar date.

As foolish as it now seems, that reiterated cliché momentarily debilitated me. I was young, immature, homesick in a foreign country—not at my mental and emotional best. I kept thinking: *I must not be a Christian, or else I would "know" when I came into the kingdom!* Then the counter-thought: *But I do know! I know when I was saved! I just do not know the "date."*

As ludicrous as it seems now, years later, that battle within me was horrendous at the time.

The distress of my spirit became such that I finally admitted to my friends in the weekly Bible study my entrenchment in the quagmire of doubt. It was a risky confession; the Americans in the group were from every part of the United States, from many different walks in life, and from a veritable smorgasbord of doctrinal opinion.

They responded readily.

11

Those from backgrounds which gave little weight to doctrine tried to encourage me: "Gene, you *know* you are a child of God!" Appreciative as I was of their confidence, such remarks were meaningless to one who realized the necessity of the new birth. Never did I redress one of those dear friends, though I knew the utter foolishness of such optimistic statements.

There must be a more definitive word from God than the mere assurance of a friend.

Some of those young men in the Thursday night Bible study were quite vigorous concerning their doctrinal tenets. They provided abundant information for every truth of Scripture we discussed. They were never without an answer—or at least an opinion. They were sincere. They *believed* what they believed!

And they believed I was lost!

Simplicity of faith is a common thread which runs among young, growing Christians; unfortunately, so is also simplicity of understanding. They had one, all-encompassing cliché which swept me into the ranks of the unconverted: "If you doubt you have been saved, it is because you never have experienced being born again!"

Just that simple. Anyone who ever had a doubt about his personal salvation was "not a Christian," else he would not be doubting. Our Thursday night Bible studies digressed into "convert Reynolds" sessions. My confession of doubt ignited a series of rapid-fire questions. Though they were grammatically couched in the form of questions, I suspected they were accusations—the fellows were attempting to "expose me to myself."

"How did you feel when you thought you were saved?"

"Did you feel different inside after you asked the Lord to save you?"

"Did you pray when you were converted?"

I answered candidly, "No. Not in the formal sense of prayer."

"How do you think you could experience salvation without praying?"

None of them took me through the Scriptures to explain what God has to say about the matter. Of course, they used isolated texts, attempting to convince me I was not a Christian. For more than six weeks this is all that took place during the Bible study periods.

I chose to desist and depart. I was being saturated with advice almost against my will. I would not believe I was truly a Christian just because my friends thought so; neither would I consider myself an unbeliever merely on the opinion of others.

I quit attending the Bible study.

But I still lived in an unsettling numbness of doubt.

Do not misunderstand. I am not accusing personal friends or visiting evangelists of disturbing my assurance. Mine was self-imposed. I had come to doubt within myself; their remarks only agitated an abiding malady. I share these experiences with you to certify that I am a fellow sufferer. I've been there myself.

In the Valley of Doubt, very little is required to produce a series of dark moments: a phrase in a hymn . . . testimonies from persons who were born again after years of assuming they were Christians . . . a verse of Scripture speaking of judgment, hypocrisy, or vain believers. . . . These will trigger an instant depression in one who is anxious about the genuineness of his salvation.

I've been there too—in the midst of such depression. Many times.

Though the period of my involuntary skepticism lasted for several months, it was not a continuous damper on my every conscious thought. There were times when I was perfectly content with my spiritual condition. It was during these times that I felt the days of uncertainty were past. They were days of delight. There were seasons when I was totally immersed in activities—some secular, some spiritual—and the "spirit of doubt" seemed to be a passive mood.

These were wonderful days! I thought peace had come!

Peace is not, however, merely the absence of tumult.

Eventually, when I was alone with myself, I would grapple once more for firm assurance of citizenship in the kingdom.

Those days of confusion proved later to be a disclosure to me of several circumstances which often prompt genuine Christians to question whether they have been born again.

First, disobedience in the Christian's life will be the seed of doubt. Disobedient Christians are "going back" on their word of commitment to the Son of God. The Scriptures offer no assurance to the one who willfully rebels against the will and way of God.

Second, lack of spiritual growth will initiate doubt in the thinking of the saint. I came to realize that lack of growth, indirectly, fostered the first seed of doubt in my mind. For ten years my life as a Christian was static. Later, I began to compare my pre-growth years with the exciting new days of renewal, and by comparison, I interpreted the days of spiritual infancy as indicative of no life at all. I *needed* the spiritual growth. It was good for me—but I did not know how to place it in proper perspective.

Third, much questioning will come to the person who seeks assurance in emotional feelings. At its very best, this kind of assurance is fluctuating.

Finally, most doubting springs ultimately from a basic misunderstanding of how we may *know* we are born again. The New Testament tells us crisply, concisely, and clearly how to be sure that we know Christ.

These are some of the common reasons for Christians doubting their salvation. Obviously, there are other reasons. The ones mentioned are not mutually exclusive of each other. Probably all of them are present to some degree in the life of the Christian who cannot find assurance.

They were present in my life.

Amid such unsure footing and confusion, why did I not simply *pray*, asking the Lord either to save me in that moment, or reveal to me that I was already a Christian? Only heaven's computers have record of how many times I prayed that prayer! It is the Doubter's Prayer—it is universal among disciples who doubt!

It all seems so simple *now*, on this side of the darkness; but it was all too complex at the time.

I meant the prayer every time I prayed it. I probably meant it *more* each time I prayed it. Never have I uttered a more serious prayer in my life! Sometimes it would be the plaintive plea of a man emotionally "drawn and wrung out"; often it was comprised of demands on our Lord: "Let me *know* if I am saved or not!"

Either way, the results were the same. Nothing.

I did not realize it then, but the "bottom line" of every prayer was for the Lord to let me "feel" I had been born again. Indeed, sometimes these were the very words I prayed. Knowing nothing of the relevant scriptural truths at this juncture, my only recourse was to "feel" saved so I could "believe" I was saved.

If I could *feel* it, I could *believe* it!

Most doubters have similar emotional excursions.

God was being so very good to me at the time. He has a more concrete way to make us sure of our salvation . . . and he was forcing me to learn it.

In the midst of my spiritual disorder I could not appreciate the "learning experience"; however, these intervening years have made me realize that our Father was not only leading me to an incontrovertible certainty of my own salvation, he was also preparing me for a "minsion into *your* assurance.

A great part of my pastoral ministry has been just that —the ministry of assurance for which he equipped me.

I could not empathize with those of you who have doubts about your spiritual life, had I not passed that way on my journey. The invasion of doubt into my assurance has made me acutely sensitive to any incursion into *your* assurance.

I've been there. I think I can help.

While no two experiences of doubting are the same, there are enough similarities which will make my journey helpful to you. Your experiences of doubting may not be as intense or as dramatic as mine were; but the underlying principles which assisted me will be helpful to you.

Now—let's take another step in our journey into assurance.

TWO
BASING ASSURANCE
ON JUST ONE EXPERIENCE

It was late in the month of January when I curtailed my fellowship with the Bible study group. In a few days, I was a recluse—physically, and in attitude.

The first week in February, our military battalion traveled to the British Zone of West Germany for anti-aircraft firing practice. We lived in tents on the shores of the Baltic Sea, near the small city of Putlos.

In order to insure the safety of the aircraft crews who towed our targets through the air, clear visibility was imperative. We stayed at the site for more than three weeks and enjoyed not one clear day; this prevented the firing practice.

The inclement weather afforded the troops an indoor vacation. I spent a great part of the time alone in a radar van, perusing the four Gospels. As I thrilled to the life and actions of the Lord Jesus, an underlying question robbed me of the full-orbed joy which ought to have come from reading of him. The question: *Was my conversion genuine?*

I vowed to maintain my private seclusion while on the Baltic in an attempt to ferret an answer to that question. I wanted assurance that my "conversion" as a child was in fact a salvation experience. I intended to turn it over and over in my mind until I determined if there was spiritual *reality* to it.

In short, I sought assurance of salvation from that one experience.

It was a mistake.

I could not find permanent assurance based on my experience of conversion—and with good reason. When the New Testament speaks to assure us of our salvation it *always* deals in the present tense; *never does it point back to the new birth experience!* The new birth is always evaluated in terms of the *present* spiritual condition.

Make no mistake—the new birth is forcefully presented in Scripture. It is extremely unwise, though, to stake our "major assurance" on something which happened at a past "point in time."

In attempting to find certainty of my salvation from my initial encounter with the Lord—turning every remembered facet of it over and over in my mind—I came to the awareness that *the years will dim the memory of the experience.* Obviously, the "facts" of the new birth will not be forgotten, but the burning intensity of the emotional circumstances fades with the passing years.

Allow me to illustrate with a "flashback."

When I was approximately ten years of age, my father introduced me to the sheriff of Dallas County—the famous "Smoot" Schmidt. The legendary lawman was known for his bravery and cunning; his name was a household word in Texas during the 1940s. It was one of the highlights of my year to meet that great man!

I shall never forget his words as he extended his hand to mine, "Son, I'm the sheriff." Every ten-year-old Texan would have been proud to meet him personally.

That was at least thirty-five years ago, and the years have dimmed the memory of that encounter. I have not spoken to Mr. Schmidt, or even seen him, since that day.

Obviously, much of what was said—and the *attendant emotions* of that hour—have long since been forgotten. It is a pleasant memory to know that I met him, but it gives no spark to my life today. His brief greeting is all I can remember from that episode. I was excited during those moments, but I cannot recall those emotions *now* as I reflect on our conversation.

If I applied the spiritual rationale of some of my friends to this situation, I might question whether I actually met the famous sheriff. I do not know the date of our meeting; I do not know how old I was at the time. You will note I mentioned I was "approximately" ten years of age. I could have been as young as eight, as old as twelve. I could ask my father and together we could compute some dates—eventually discerning my age at the time. This would not, however, alter the facts. I *did* meet Sheriff Schmidt of Dallas County when I was a youngster, though time has erased some of the details.

The same is true of my conversion.

I came to Christ as a youngster; I still do not know the date of the experience. For many years I thought I was ten years of age at the time. My mother has contended I was nine. My friend Bobby Bryan—converted just two weeks before me—insists we were only eight years old.

Again, it would be a simple matter to check the church records for the date. Then I would know my age at the time—except that it is of relative unimportance.

Time does have an *eroding* effect on the memory of events. Many details will escape the mind, and nothing can bring back the identical set of emotional circumstances. Too much fades with the passing years. For us to place our sole confidence for salvation on a past encounter is to possess a withering, uncertain assurance.

Allow me to share three points concerning my conversion to Christ.

First, I remember the setting. It was in a morning worship service of the Seevers Street Baptist Church in

Dallas. There are three sections of pews in the sanctuary: I sat in the right section, the first row, the left end. I was less than fifteen feet from the pulpit.

Second, I remember the Spirit of God speaking to me. Though I did not understand who he was at the time, I knew a force greater than myself had spoken to me in an unusual way. I thought of it as any youngster would have: "Jesus spoke to my heart." I knew I needed Christ in my life.

I responded publicly, and the tension within me was relieved as I moved toward the altar. I believe I was converted when I took that first step. It was a faith response to Christ. Pastor Harvey L. Nelson asked if I wanted to receive Jesus as my Savior. I affirmed that I did. We did not pray in the formal sense, but my public response was to Christ! A counselor came to me as I was seated and asked, "Gene, do you want to join the church and be baptized?" I recall thinking to myself, "There is more to it than that!"

Third, I remember the only concept I had about becoming a Christian was that of receiving Christ into my life. I did not think that water baptism, church membership, or anything else could save me. I had been taught that Christ alone could save.

This was my simple—but transforming—experience of receiving Jesus Christ into my life.

In my period of doubting, I did not question that *something* happened to me that day—I just wondered what! I also did not question that God had in reality spoken to me during that worship service—*I just wondered if I had made the correct response!*

I have not talked with the sheriff of Dallas County since being introduced to him that day, so the meeting is dimmer with the passing of time. I *have* had fellowship with Jesus Christ during the more than thirty-five years I have known him, but even so, the "experience" of my new birth is not as clearly in focus now as it was in the early months following it.

No matter how emotionally explosive, how dramatic or traumatic your new birth may have been, to look upon it for your *chief* assurance of salvation is to reach for an assurance which is slowly fading.

Those days and nights huddled around an electric heater on the cold Baltic shores were spent in an attempt to reconstruct my initial encounter with Christ.

The irony of it is that though I was able to remember so very many of the details of the conversion itself, I was not at all satisfied.

I finally realized the problem: I had been seeking to reconstruct the *emotions* of that moment. Again, this seems to be universal among Christians who are doubting their salvation.

Admittedly, there would be some measure of certainty concerning our salvation in being able to call back the joy and other attendant emotions of the day we were born again. But it is not possible. Time does obscure and shadow the memory, even of things spiritual.

After isolating myself for the first week we were on the Baltic, I began to fellowship once more with my friends in the battalion. Though I did not consciously plan to do it, I soon found myself asking some of the Christian fellows to share their conversion experiences with me.

Without knowing it, I had fallen into another of those traps we doubters fail to recognize—*comparing conversions!*

One of the chief agitations of doubt among the saints comes from the vivid testimonies we hear. In our evangelical churches we give much attention to "personal testimonies" of conversion—and well we should! It is a wonderful encouragement to both saint and sinner to hear a layperson tell of a vibrant, firsthand encounter with the living Christ.

Yet these same testimonials, while inspiriting both believer and unbeliever, may be inadvertently sources of confusion for Christians who are in the midst of doubting their personal salvation.

The reason? That human tendency to compare conversions. *"But mine was not like that!"*

Listening to my friends share their testimonies—while still attempting to find assurance out of my conversion experience—I began comparing my new birth circumstances with theirs, as if *theirs* was the standard pattern for mine!

I listened to the testimony of a soldier friend who had possessed some doctrinal grasp of Christianity before he gave his life to Christ. His boyhood had been filled with physical debilitations: he had only one kidney and was the victim of a rare disease as a boy. His maladies had made him bitter against God as a youth.

He told me of the "writhing in his soul" for months before he allowed the Lord to save him. He spoke of *wrestling* with the Holy Spirit; of his conscious rejection of the Son of God. He then employed the term "regeneration" to explain that he had accepted God's gift of "new life."

Ignoring the fact that he had been reared in a Bible-believing home, and that he was twenty-one years of age before he was born again, I began to compare my simple conversion to his.

When I received Christ into my life I was like those men whom Paul accosted at Athens—I did not know whether there was a Holy Spirit (Acts 19). I knew nothing about the regenerating work of the Spirit of God when I made my profession of faith—but that young man did!

I wondered—*maybe I was not saved at the first!*

I attempted to foist that term "regeneration" into the setting of my own salvation experience. It merely bred added perplexity. Can you imagine a ten-year-old realizing—even before his conversion—*that he needed to know the regenerating work of the Spirit of God in his life . . . in order to effect the new birth within his nature?*

Comparing conversions did for me what it does for most others who do it: It added to my spiritual frustration.

Other servicemen told of the great sin in their lives, and of the deep, deep guilt they sensed before coming to Christ. I had not sensed such deep guilt. I had not felt the "weight of sin" upon me as others had. Try as I did, I could not remember that I had a conscious understanding of the poignant sense of immorality, etc., before coming to Christ.

I knew at my conversion that I was a sinner, but a young boy is not familiar with the vices of life to which he will unfortunately later be exposed. My recurring thought during those days on the Baltic: Since I had not known these things when I had my youthful experience, perhaps I was not actually reborn.

I was just a young man during those horrendous months of doubt. I had yet to learn that every human personality is different, that every human situation has distinct circumstances. Each person's birth is unique—the attendant emotions, the intellectual grasp, even the resoluteness of the will. The backgrounds of people coming to Christ are widely diversified—the varying intensity of guilt, the divergent feelings of incompleteness, the differing levels in recognition of need.

There are persons who were grossly immoral and degenerate—who came to Christ after years of running from God, their conscience, and perhaps the law of the land. My life was not like that, so my experience with Christ was different; not at all inferior, just different.

This tendency to "compare conversions" is rampant among Christians who doubt their salvation. Since it is such a venomous infection—inflicting near-irreparable damage on some seekers after assurance—it needs to be laid to rest "once and for all."

Allow me to share the setting of two *contrasting* conversions. This will further illustrate the folly of comparing our spiritual birth with that of someone else.

There is a gentleman in our church by the name of William Elwood Bogan. He was converted to Christ in the living room of his home in April of 1968. Suffering skips in his heartbeat, he thought he was going to die; so he called for a friend to tell him how to be saved.

On the Tuesday he was born again, he wept in joyous relief, and asked the four others present with him to sing "What Can Wash Away My Sin?" The scene portrayed one of those seizures of emotion so powerful that none of them could move their lips, let alone utter audible sounds. It is an understatement to say that he had an "emotional" experience.

William Elwood Bogan is a choice friend. Several times, in evangelistic campaigns, I have invited him to give the testimony of his conversion to Christ. It never fails to "move" an audience.

I recount some of the background of his spiritual birth.

A native of North Carolina, he grew up in a Christian home. His mother took him to every revival meeting in the county when he was a youth, but he wanted no part of being a Christian. He left home at an early age and became a career Marine. His life in the military led him to all parts of the globe and into most of the temptations of the world.

He became an obsessive gambler—everything he did in life had a wager riding on it. His manner of living was alien to the life in Christ, and he had not even the slightest interest in the Son of God. His was a haggard hostility to the gospel. It took the fright of heart failure to awaken him to the gentle voice of the Holy Spirit.

His crossing of the Great River into life was totally unlike mine.

24

He did not want to endure the "pangs" of the crossing. It was difficult for him to start through the waters. His lifelong reluctance to the gospel message forced him farther and farther down the secular shore. He entered the river at its widest, deepest point. While he was making his way through the surging currents, the waves lashed at his head—nearly overcoming him several times. The depth of the river was almost more than he could ford.

His own rebellion made it a treacherous crossing. He thought of all he was leaving on the secular shore—the friends, the good times, the zest of life. Even during the crossing itself, he thought of turning back. As he neared the Shore of Life, the waves became increasingly more vicious. The prodding providence of God and the ceaseless tugging of the Holy Spirit were all that kept him moving toward life's shore.

Finally, drenched—emotionally wrenched—he made it! He was *safe* in the kingdom. Few conversions have been as emotional, as dramatic.

My own crossing was different. I moved through the river when I was "about ten"; William Bogan was thirty years older at the time of his crossing. He had spent years in a life of sin; my life had hardly begun.

My friend refused the call of God many times before he gave his life to Christ. Because I did not refuse his call even one time, I intersected the river at its narrowest, most shallow point. The waters were deep for my friend; I merely waded through the shoals. Though the waters lashed at his head, they lapped gently at my feet. His crossing was intensely emotional; mine was not.

But when I stepped out of that river, I was nonetheless *safe* on the Shore of Life.

William Bogan and I are both in the kingdom of our God and of Christ—I'm as secure in my salvation as he is.

My experience can be identical to that of no one. So

comparing mine with another will not bring assurance
. . . it most often brings frustration.

As I moved among the professing Christians in our camp
on the Baltic, I came to the realization, even then, that I
would not find assurance of my salvation by looking
back to my new birth encounter.

I have shared two thoughts with you concerning the
folly of reaching back to the conversion experience for
assurance of salvation: *the years dimming the memory of
the experience* and *the frustration we feel in comparing conversions with other people.*

There is a third thought. *Some religious "conversions"
are spurious, counterfeit.* No conversion experience is able
to stand alone, on its own authority; it must come under
the scrutiny of the written Word of God!

One veteran soldier shared his testimony with me,
unsolicited on my part. His eyes welled with tears as he
told of the day of his "conversion"; it was the "greatest
day" of his life.

The man was a drunkard, dishonest in his personal
dealings, an inveterate liar. His way of life was open; he
enjoyed the anti-Christian life he had adopted. He had no
plans to change any of his ways. He cursed the church of
the living Lord; he made fun of it—he "had no need for
it."

He hated all ministers of the Christ whom he claimed
to know.

But he had experienced "conversion."

I was in a wretched spiritual condition myself, but I
remember thinking that I would not have traded places
with that man!

Jesus said it succinctly: *We will be able to recognize spiritual genuineness in people (including ourselves!) by the fruit
which is evident in those lives* (Matt. 7:16).

Again, it is important to note that the new birth always
is evaluated by the life it produces. Looking at that life in

the light of the New Testament, we are able to trace back through the years the expressions of the fruit of Christ in our lives. Then we are able to ascertain if what happened in the beginning was true conversion.

There is a rationale behind this meandering presentation. I have wanted you to see from every perspective that a fixation on the new birth "experience" for one who is doubting can be calamitous. If you find assurance on this journey we are taking together, it will happen only after you have released that fixation.

Do not base your hope for assurance on just one experience in the past. God has a more definitive plan, a more certain plan of assurance for you!

I had gone to the Baltic encampment at Putlos with strong determination to find assurance out of my own salvation experience. I did not find it. As we were breaking camp for the trip back to our home base in Wiesbaden, I was a disappointed young man; but like Edison and his light bulb, I had discovered one way we *cannot* find assurance.

I was not giving up. My journey into assurance would last a few months longer before I would come to the fruitful end of it.

Meanwhile, exhausted from the strain of my inner turmoil, I thought how good it would be someday to "feel" saved.

THREE
TRYING TO "FEEL" SAVED

On the first Saturday evening following our return from the Baltic, I attended the Youth for Christ rally in Wiesbaden. Our guest speaker for that night was a warm-hearted evangelical missionary to the Germans.

He seemed genuinely concerned about people, and that encouraged me to talk with him in private after the close of the service. I shared with him that I had no assurance of the genuineness of my conversion to Christ. I quickly told him of my profession of faith as a youngster, of the college year, of the months of doubt. He was an engaging, exciting fellow, and after we had talked for about ten minutes he interrogated, "Gene do you really *know* Christ?"

That's why I had come to him, because I was uncertain if I actually *knew* Christ! Under the circumstances of our conversation it would have been humiliating to give anything but an affirmative answer. I replied that I did.

He turned to 2 Timothy 1:12 and read to me: "I know whom I have believed, and I am convinced that he is able to guard what I have entrusted to him until that day."

Once more he forcefully questioned, "Now—do you really *know* Christ?"

This time I answered readily, "Yes!"

He reached for my hand and placed it on that verse of Scripture, while breaking into an emotional prayer. The essence of that prayer was that I could have confidence in Christ to keep that which I had entrusted to him. During the prayer he placed a fatherly grasp on my shoulder and gently squeezed it. At the conclusion of the prayer he grabbed my hand to shake it. As he vigorously pumped it a dozen times, he uttered a deeply felt, "God bless you," and admonished me to take God at his Word!

I left for the Wiesbaden Air Base "feeling" great! I remembered the song based on that Scripture, and I hummed it all the way to the barracks—"I Know Whom I Have Believed."

The "feeling" of assurance wore off before I went to bed that night. Assurance which rests solely on emotional feelings usually lasts for a very brief period, then disappears as vapor. When that happens, it usually leaves the doubter in a more depressed state than before the "assurance" came.

I was not consciously attempting to "feel" saved, as much as I was trying to keep from feeling "unsaved." Those dagger-like thrusts of emotional fear which a doubter experiences are mentally ravaging; they paralyze us spiritually.

I wanted to escape as many of those experiences as possible.

This matter of emotional feelings is a constant temptation for those of us who want to enjoy our walk in the Lord. Through the years of my ministry I have heard the same statement reiterated again and again—as a matter of fact, I have said it myself many times. The essence of it is: "I wanted to 'feel' it, so I'll know it is real!" Different people mean different things by the remark, but the "bottom line" is that we want to sense the very presence of God within us.

I wanted to "sense his presence" on the evening I talked with the evangelical missionary, and he inadvertently assisted me in my search for an emotional feeling. The question he asked of me—"Gene, do you really *know* Christ?"—was not based on any New Testament statement. He read from the Scriptures only *after* he had received an answer to his question. His whole thrust of communication was in the emotional appeal of his voice. The missionary is a Christian gentleman, sound and sincere. He did not mislead me; he attempted to encourage me in the Lord. I simply did not have the biblical foundation which he assumed I possessed.

It is a common malady among us to base assurance of our salvation on feelings of emotion. One of the more subtle avenues of it is to employ the use of Scripture as a "basis" for the sensation of assurance.

One of my friends in the Thursday night Bible study took a special interest in me. He had a choleric temperament and went "straight to the heart" of every issue he discussed. During a conversation in my barracks room one evening he paced the floor dogmatically, spouting New Testament verses to me. He fully intended that I would come to the assurance of my salvation "that night"!

He would quote evangelistic texts, then ask authoritatively, "Do you believe *that*?" I believed every one of them, and after each of my affirmations he would emphatically intone, "Then you are *SAVED!*" The way he thundered each time he used the word "saved" got me excited. Maybe I *was!*

The last verse he used in his admirably sincere approach to my assurance was John 6:37, from the words of the Lord Jesus himself: "The one who comes to Me I will certainly not cast out."

He demanded: "Will the Lord cast you out?" No. "If he doesn't cast you out, then what *does* he do?"

I didn't know exactly how to answer, and when I

hesitated, he supplied the response for me: "He keeps you in, right?"

What could I say? I answered yes.

"Then you are *SAVED!*"

Now I had some "scriptural" assurance. It lasted until he left my room. I knew Christ would not cast me out if I came to him, but my basic question remained: *"Had I come to him?"* Again, though we discussed many marvelous declarations from God's Word, the half hour's assurance I gained was founded on his energetically emotional presentation—not on the New Testament.

During the month of March I became immersed in so many enjoyable activities that I "felt good" about myself, and the days of questioning my conversion were not as intense as they had been during the winter months.

In the first week of the month my roommate and I purchased a fifteen-year-old Mercedes. It had no battery in it when we bought it, and we had to push the car to get it started. It was one of the few automobiles among the men in our battalion, and we enjoyed celebrity status for a few weeks.

Since we had to push the car to get it started, some of our friends declined to socialize with us, protesting they were "physically unable" to travel with us. We sought to find parking spaces on hilltops in order to start the car with less physical exertion. Those were good days for me. The laughing, traveling, and the nonsense involved with the Mercedes lightened my spirit.

The softball season began in the early days of the same month and provided a relief from the tenuousness of military service in a foreign nation. The team was privileged to have time away from the regular daily duties. The break in routine was refreshingly welcome, especially after a severe winter had kept us from the competitive sports. Again, my own spirits were heightened, and the confusion concerning my personal salvation was at least temporarily removed from the forefront of my every conscious thought.

I spent Easter weekend in Paris. "April in Paris" was like walking in a history book. Seeing some of the historical monuments, plus the general splendor of one of the great cities of the world, proved an aid to me in restoring some elasticity to my strained emotions.

I had stayed away from the Saturday night Youth for Christ rallies all during the month of March, so I did not have any "evangelistic encounters" for a period of five or six weeks. I am aware now that perhaps I did not act wisely during those days, but I had been overwhelmed emotionally in those "assurance sessions."

I did need a break from those well-meaning friends of mine!

In mid-April several of us from Wiesbaden went to a Sunday evening Youth for Christ rally in Frankfurt, thirty miles away. We made the trip in our Mercedes, still without a battery. The Frankfurt rally was conducted on Sunday evenings in an Army chapel in the very heart of the city. The chapel had a large grand piano and a powerful organ.

We arrived thirty minutes before the service started, and the refrains of gospel hymns met us as we entered the building. I had not heard instruments played like that since I had left Texas! The singing in the service was moving, militant. With my emotions now relaxed, I could enjoy the service. I was caught up quickly in the music portion of the service and thoroughly enjoyed myself. As we fervently sang the great hymns of our faith, I realized I was "feeling good" about my salvation.

The "feelings" lasted longer than the previous assurances I had gathered, because I sang to myself for a week. I literally sang myself into assurance. Surely no one would enjoy those songs as much as I was enjoying them if he were not saved!

That certainty of salvation went the way of all "manipulated assurance"; within two weeks I was back to where I had begun. It is always like that when we base assurance solely on emotional feelings.

I have already shared with you concerning the two-month period when I was quite pointedly "trying to feel saved." The truth is, however, that all through those months I was doubting my salvation, there was a subconscious desire to have "feelings" of assurance. In the testimonies I heard, almost without exception, there was a reference to how great it feels to be saved.

I wanted to feel great about "my" salvation—enjoy it as so many others seemed to do. This desire left me "wide open" to those unpredictable emotions. When functioning alone, unchecked by the other faculties, they run rampant in all directions. The spiritual instability which resulted in my life was a very poor presentation of the unchanging Christ who lives in me.

Sometimes my emotions would droolingly slather spiritual bubble all over me, and I would have the boisterous swagger of a high-born child of the King. Because of a natural tendency to arrogance, when my emotions encouraged me toward one of those "spiritual highs," I had enough confidence to walk on water. A hundred mustard seeds could not have equaled my faith! During those times of unparalleled boldness it is a wonder I did not remove some of those European mountains, casting them into the sea!

In other seasons—often before I would realize it was happening—my overworked emotions would drain me of all "spiritual energy." The numbness which followed caused me to be dull and listless—and uninterested—concerning the things of God. While such a fluctuating faith did not cause me to oscillate ethically and morally, it did harm my testimony with the unbelievers in my battalion.

It also proved to be quite frustrating to *me*.

The word "feelings" is not found in the Bible. The New Testament never draws on emotions as a source for assurance of salvation. *Never.* The Scripture does not, however, negate emotions as a legitimate part of our psychological makeup.

We do possess emotions. They are an intricate part of our total being. Men of scholarship will vary in their descriptions of the emotions, but all seem to agree that the emotions are integrated into complex coordination with the mental and physical faculties. It is not good for any one of the faculties to function apart from the other two—to function alone. While emotions are important —indeed, *necessary*—it is best that they function in harmony with the mental and the physical.

If the emotions function alone it means they are functioning without facts—without proper data. This is unwise in any instance, in any area of our lives; however, it can be more than "unwise" in the spiritual realm; it can be deadly!

The coordinated use of the emotions with the mental and physical faculties is understood better in other areas than the spiritual. All of us have our own prejudices concerning the spiritual area; often we are less than objective.

A few years ago my favorite professional football team was involved in a playoff game. A defeat would have meant the disappointing end to their season; a victory meant playing in the Super Bowl. With only seconds remaining in the game, my emotional state was one of deepest gloom. "My team" appeared to be a certain loser. Suddenly, without the slightest hint of what was going to happen, they bolted to a touchdown and snatched a dramatic victory from the other team.

My son and I were watching the game together. Our

gloom-filled emotions immediately became super-charged with the thrill of victory. Both of us let out "war whoops" of emotional joy and celebration. The unexpected victory was such an enjoyable "shock" to us that we joined arms and did a goose-stepping march around the room, our voices at a high decibeled pitch. The more we relived that "last-ditch touchdown," the more we enjoyed it; the more we enjoyed it, the louder we became in our accolades to the team and its coach.

Finally, my always-in-control wife came into the room to tell us that our noise would cause the neighbors to think we had "lost our minds." When her down-to-earth reminder did not dampen our shrill enthusiasm, she reprimanded us with one of those wifely ultimatums: *"For goodness' sake, settle down!"* Her joy had been tempered with common sense, self-control, etc. Mine was temporarily without restraint.

An hour later, all of that unabated joy had subsided into a quiet, peaceful inner glow as I conversed with a friend about how "our boys" had done it again. The joy was still as deep, as real as it had been earlier, but it was better coordinated with my mental faculties. Though the emotional excitement died away within a few days, through the years I often have feasted mentally on the memory of that last-minute touchdown.

In the days preceding the Super Bowl, I had "full assurance" that my favorite team would play for the world championship; but it was not merely an emotional assurance.

There is a euphemism we evangelicals have utilized for many years to describe the coordination of the emotions with the other faculties. It is *fact, faith, feeling.* If these three words were placed on a blackboard for visual aid, the words would be written in the form of a train. *Fact* is the engine; it pulls the train. *Faith* is the fuel car which is joined to the engine—to the fact. *Feeling* is the caboose.

The rather obvious application is that the caboose does not pull the train.

In our coordination of the emotions with the rest of our faculties, *feeling* does not "pull the train of assurance." It is always last! My assurance concerning my favorite team playing in the Super Bowl was not founded on emotion, but on fact. The *fact* was that the team had won the previous playoff game. No amount of *emotional* assurance would have placed them in the Super Bowl, but the *fact* of their victory in the preceding game did.

I also had *faith*—but in the facts. No amount of my faith would have put the team in the championship game. Faith does not create facts; it *responds* to them!

Since I knew the facts and had faith in them, my *feelings* were not functioning alone; they were in harmony with my other faculties. My team was not going to the Super Bowl just because I "felt good" about them.

When we allow our emotions to be the sole source of our assurance of salvation, we face this problem: The emotions ebb and flow, rise up and die down. When the emotions are at a low ebb, we have nothing else to which we can cling for assurance.

In our search for assurance of spiritual life, we must apply the principle of fact, faith, feeling. It is an imperative. Such an approach will gently prohibit us from relying *only* on our feelings.

The simple fact-faith-feeling principle provides us with competent assistance in securing our assurance. What God speaks to us in his Word is *fact*. We are to place our *faith* in God's *fact*; not in our *feelings*. God's fact is true, even if we do not believe; however, when we do believe, the "feelings" of satisfaction will follow. It should always be in that order: fact, faith, feeling. When emotional feelings are in their proper place, they are in healthy coordination with the other faculties.

With our emotions functioning properly, we will indeed "feel good" about our salvation, and the feelings will have stability and permanence to them.

I want to share the testimony of a fellow soldier who had an *unemotional* experience of conversion to Christ. I shall call him Frank.

When I came to a settled assurance of my own salvation, I began to share my faith in Christ with the men in my work area. The first time I mentioned the Lord to Frank he informed me that the work area was no place to have a Sunday school lesson.

But he listened.

Though he did not respond often with words, it became obvious that he was paying close attention to everything I had to say. The casually brief conversations lasted for several weeks. Though I knew he was listening intently, I did not realize he was close to conversion.

I was given a brief assignment in another city, and due to the nature of it, I was not in communication with any of the men in my battalion. I was away for more than a month. Upon my return I first saw Frank after an evening meal. He had spotted me in the dining hall and was waiting for me just outside—a menacing glare on his face, his attitude militant.

"Reynolds," he blurted, "I asked God to save me and he didn't do it!"

My youthful immaturity surfaced, and I said, "Well, you ought to feel honored! You're probably the first sinner in history Christ has refused!"

"I'm serious, Reynolds. I did everything you told me to do," he thundered in a tone which indicated he was not only quite serious, but in emotional agony.

I began retracing his steps. "When did you ask the Lord to save you?"

"About two weeks ago."

"Were you serious about it?"

"You know I was or I wouldn't be here right now! I've been looking for you to come back every day since then."

We stepped behind the dining hall building for privacy.

We talked through matters of vital import. Did he give himself to Christ totally? Had he been willing for Christ to be the supreme Lord of his life? Did he truly repent? Did he trust in Christ, and Christ alone, for his salvation?

My interrogation lasted for half an hour. His answer to every question was an emphatic "yes." During that lengthy and reiterated period of questioning, I prepared some verbal daggers to thrust at my friend—with a view to his spiritual healing.

"Frank, you have told me about living in a Christian home, about your mother's encouraging words to you concerning Christ, and of your plans to 'someday' become a Christian. During this period in which I have talked with you, you have planned to be born again, haven't you?"

With his affirmative answer, I became bolder.

"You have looked with relish toward the day of your planned conversion, thought how good it would feel, of the joy you would have, of how happy you would be to know that your sins were forgiven. Isn't this true?"

"To a degree, yes."

"Frank, let me tell you something. You claim you were sincere in asking Christ to save you. I believe you. And I believe something else. I believe he *did* save you, Frank, and you are disappointed with the way he has brought it to pass! You didn't have the emotional quakes you had envisioned! You didn't have the great *feeling* you had dreamed about! Christ has *saved* you and you are not satisfied with the emotional circumstances of it!"

We stood silent, motionless, staring at each other. I was fearful I had said the wrong thing—and too much of it.

It seemed he glared at me for an angry eternity. Slowly, the glare gave way to a grin. Even more slowly, the grin was transformed into a warm glow.

Finally, he spoke. "You know, Gene, I really *am* saved, and this is the first time I've realized it! I kept waiting to *feel* saved . . . but since I've just let go to believe it I *do* feel saved."

He worded it better in a few days. He told me that at first he put his faith in his feelings, rather than in his Savior.

It is always first fact . . . then faith . . . then feeling.

Still another unemotional conversion serves to illuminate our thinking concerning "feelings."

Just a few years ago I conducted an evangelistic week at a Christian college in Texas. During the course of the week I had several conversations with a young woman who desperately wanted to become a Christian. Her eternal salvation—in her mind—hinged on her having a certain "feeling" before she could be born again.

The "feeling" had been eluding her for several years —through many such weeks of revival emphasis.

Late in the week, in frustration with her, I offered these words: "Mary, just as surely as you plan a certain set of emotions to attend your conversion, God will bring it about in another way."

My comments shocked her, for the emotions connected with the new birth had been the center of our every conversation.

I submitted a rationale for my statement. Had she not, in her years of waiting for that "right feeling," thought how rich would be her future moment of conversion? Had she not been thrilled emotionally at the prospect of being born again? She admitted this to be true. The anticipated "feeling" was the deepest longing of her heart.

I projected my reasoning more specifically. She would reflect back on her conversion experience in the future, remembering how she had dreamed of it, even planned it. Doubts would come. The question would then arise in her thinking whether she had been transformed through the process of spiritual birth; or if she had simply employed "emotional manipulation." I still recall my last statement to her, "So that you will enjoy full assurance of your salvation twenty years from now, the Heavenly Father will arrange for emotional circumstances other than you have planned."

She accepted my explanation—intellectually, at least.

In the chapel service on the last day of that week, Mary responded to the invitation appeal, giving her life to Christ.

I did not realize until after the service that she was among those who were converted. She sought me out before leaving the chapel, sharing this testimony: "I told God I was ready to become a Christian, that I would take him at his Word, even if I never received any particular *feeling*. From the moment I prayed those words, the peace I had always wanted—it came!"

It is always fact, then faith, then feeling.

Mary referred to the last word as "peace."

While I was on my journey through the "wilderness of Wiesbaden," I had not yet come to know that "faith" is a much greater word than "feeling."

I was coming to learn that I could not find assurance based on my emotional feelings.

I didn't care how I gained assurance; I just wanted it!

It was good for me to call to mind a verse of Scripture from somewhere in the Old Testament. That was the closest I could come to locating it. It was a promise from God that when we seek him with all of our heart . . . we will find him.

I directed my heart fully to seek him for either assurance or salvation. I would "hold on" to that promise that I remembered from "somewhere in the Old Testament."

It had been a good spring for me in Wiesbaden. I had at least eliminated another way that one cannot find assurance.

Better days were ahead.

FOUR
LEARNING THE VITAL SIGNS

The fifth month of the year brought fresh adventure and launched me toward new insights in my quest for assurance.

May 1 is regarded as International Labor Day by most of Europe. The "May Day" celebrations brought out the Germans in capacious numbers, especially congesting their major traffic thoroughfares. Though military personnel were vigorously admonished to remain on the fringes of the festivities, my roommate and I were in the thick of the crowds, and were involved in a late evening automobile accident.

Our "new" fifteen-year-old Mercedes was totally demolished in a collision with an automobile occupied by three members of the United States Navy. Their Rhine River Patrol was headquartered close to Wiesbaden, and the sailors were a part of the patrol operation.

One of the Navy men was critically injured and was rushed to the Twelfth Air Force General Hospital in Wiesbaden. Anxious because of our kindred spirit with a fellow American, we stayed the night just outside the intensive care unit where the young man spent hours hovering between life and death.

His commanding officer was alerted; he hurried to the

hospital to keep the vigil with us. I listened intently to the muted conversations between the physicians and the commanding officer. It seemed that during every medical briefing there were references to the "vital signs." Joyous relief came the next day when a nurse reported to us that his vital signs were approaching *normal* readings, indicating stability.

It was the first time in my life that I had consciously given attention to the importance of the *vital signs.*

Over the next two months, two or three friends were in the hospital for very brief stays. During visits with them I noted the nurses diligently kept records of the vital signs. I was learning that they are accurate indicators of one's physical condition.

In the summer months that followed, I was introduced to the small epistle of 1 John. I had read in it only once or twice in my life, so I knew nothing of this short book. A gifted Presbyterian chaplain suggested that John lists some of the "birthmarks" of the Christian—spiritual birthmarks!

The chaplain's recommendation ignited my interest in the small New Testament book. I began to study it thoroughly, seriously looking for those birthmarks. My own immaturity, however, disallowed the term "birthmarks" from any desirable connotation. I could only think of imperfect skin pigmentation or surface discoloration in relation to the birthmarks—the concept simply would not "jell" in my mind.

Searching through the book proved to be a catalyst for my mental process. Rather than "birthmarks," I began to note what I first called "signs" of spiritual life. It was not long after that I noted on the margin of my Bible alongside 1 John 3:14 that it was a "spiritual vital sign." No great spark of illumination came to me in that moment, but from that time forward I employed the term with consistency.

I believe it is an accurate explanation of what John is

44

saying to us. The apostle gives consideration to these "signs" to help us have certainty of our eternal salvation —this is his motive for mentioning them so frequently. He realizes that our assurance of being born again must rest on something *outside* of ourselves. Our assurance is to rest, not in feelings or experiences, but in what God has told us in his written Word.

It was good for me to "live" in the book of 1 John. The author writes carefully, clearly—that we may understand the "vital signs" of our spiritual life.

Since there is an intriguing parallel between our "spiritual" vital signs and our physical ones, let us first consider the physical signs in order to illustrate more fully 'he parallel between the two. The physical vital signs are ive: pulse beat, blood pressure, respiration, temperature, pupillary reflex.

Pulse beat. As blood is pumped by the heart, it travels through the artery system in pulsations that match the heartbeat. The wavelike motion it produces is easily felt on the skin surface. The human pulse is usually counted at the radial artery of the wrist. When the heart functions normally, the pulse rate indicates it with approximately seventy beats per minute.

Blood pressure. This vital sign reveals the pressure of the blood in the artery system. Though there are several variations of "standard" blood pressure, it is generally conceded that 120-over-80 is normal. The upper reading, called *systolic*, represents blood pressure when the heart is contracting; the lower, or *diastolic*, indicates blood pressure when the heart is relaxing. Blood pressure tells a physician volumes about a person's health.

Respiration. The "breathing rate" is sixteen per minute when we are awake. Under strain it will be much higher. One "breath" is the cycle of inhaling oxygen and exhaling carbon dioxide. There is probably less variation related to this vital sign than any of the others. The respiratory count is simply sixteen.

45

Body temperature. The balance of body heat is ninety-eight to ninety-nine degrees. Though some persons ordinarily have a slightly lower or higher temperature, it seldom is more than one degree removed from the "normal" register. Much variation from the ninety-eight to ninety-nine degree range signifies some form of internal disorder. Body temperature is perhaps the simplest of the vital signs to detect.

Pupillary reflex. Note how often a physician looks into the eyes of a patient. Many times he shines a light into the eye. There is good reason. The iris of the eye contracts when light shines directly upon it. *The contraction is indicative of the sensitivity of the brain.* The contraction of the iris is a good sign.

It is important to note that the vital signs are merely indicators—organic meters. They do not *cause* the existing internal condition, they only report that the condition exists.

And they are accurate.

The five vital signs are inextricably related. If one of them indicates "life," so will the other four. If there is a blood pressure, there will be a heartbeat, etc. If there is absolutely no blood pressure, none of the other signs will give a reading of "life." As indicators of life they are interrelated.

They will not contradict one another.

The fascinating comparison between the physical and the spiritual vital signs thrusts a floodlight of meaning into the concept of assurance. The spiritual signs I discovered in 1 John are five: commitment to the lordship of Christ; possession of a new nature; confession of Jesus as Lord; possession of the Holy Spirit; possession of a love for Christians.

Commitment to the lordship of Christ. John refers several times to "keeping his commandments." This refers to the whole of the written Word as well as personal obedience to "impression commands" which come from his

Holy Spirit. We shall see that John is not speaking merely of a dutiful abiding by some moral code, but of willful obedience to the Son of God and to the teachings of his written Word. This rules out the "good moral person" concept.

If we are willing to obey the Lord in every aspect of his commandments for our lives, it is an evidence that we have been born again.

Possession of a new nature. Those of us who have been converted to Christ have a "new" nature. We do not effect such a change within ourselves—God does it! John makes very bold assertions that our changed nature is a positive vital sign, indicating we possess the life of God within us.

Our new nature is a clear, ringing premise that we have been saved.

Confession of Jesus as Lord. The necessity of our confessing Jesus Christ as Lord is reiterated again and again throughout the New Testament. It comes to us from the eloquent statements of our Lord, from the polished pen of Paul, and from the poignant, penetrating thought of John. If we have come to know Jesus Christ within we are not able to contain it; his presence within us *compels* us to confess him to others.

If we are willing to confess that he is not only *the* Lord, but *our* Lord—this is confirmation of conversion.

Possession of the Holy Spirit. John cogently declares that we can know we are in Christ, and Christ in us, because he has given the Holy Spirit to live in us. If the Spirit of God lives in us, we are children of God; if he does not live in us, it is evidence that we have not been born again.

The Holy Spirit within is a vital sign which registers a definitive line of demarcation between the saved and the unsaved.

Possession of a love for Christians. Perhaps the most incisive statement of assurance in all of the New Testament comes from John's pen: "We know that we have passed out of death into life, because we love the brethren" (3:14). What a forceful word of assurance! If we genuinely love all Christians, it means God has already done a saving work within us. We *already* have passed out of spiritual death and into spiritual life!

There is salient clarity here. If we love all Christians, it is a demonstration of the life of God within us.

It is important to note, of these spiritual vital signs, that which is also true of the physical ones—they are only indicators. Again, they do not *cause* the existing conditions; they report that the conditions exist! They are external symptoms of what is inside.

As with the physical signs, these spiritual ones are correlated to each other. If one of them indicates "life," so will the others. If we have the Holy Spirit living within us, we also have a new nature, a special love for Christians, etc. Contrariwise, if one of the vital signs reads "no life," the others will agree. If we do not have the Holy Spirit living within us, there will be no evidence of a new nature, etc.

The spiritual vital signs will never contradict each other.

And they are accurate.

In my own experience that summer in Germany, as I studied what John had to say about these evidences of spiritual life, I had no trouble understanding what he writes to us. It was not difficult to ponder his remarks, then categorize the vital signs into several areas. As a matter of fact, I was able to do it in just a few days.

The "bare truth" was not a problem to grasp. The idea of personalizing it for myself was the problem.

Since I had found nothing in John's epistle about the new birth experience, or about feelings, I was forced to interpret my own spiritual condition in the light of the signal information at hand—those vital signs!

The interrogations in my mind seemed endless. OK, if the Spirit of God lives in me, I am born again.

But how may I know for sure the Holy Spirit does live in me?

How do I know these impressions I have are from God? Are they "Spirit impressions"? How can I be sure?

Sometimes I feel good, happy, even joyful. But maybe I am just being positive about life. I know some people who do not even claim to be Christians, yet they have a happy outlook on life. *So how can I be sure if the Spirit actually lives in me?*

Other questions bombarded me.

If the Holy Spirit does live in me, why am I so miserable at times? Where is all this joy I hear people talk about? Where is all the peace the Spirit gives?

How can anyone know for sure that the Spirit lives in him?

I wondered if I loved Christians the way John means. I fully grasped the meaning, I just did not know if I "measured up."

The questions kept coming.

Sure, I love Christians, but a lot of these men in the Army are not Christians, and I love them—what is the difference between loving Christians and loving non-Christians? In attempting to be honest with myself about Christian love, I confused myself.

I had been converted at the age of ten. How could I know, years later, whether I had had my nature changed at conversion? What was I like before my nature was changed?

Countless numbers of questions were in my mind continuously concerning these evidences of being born again.

I needed some time alone.

I knew that we were scheduled for a trip back to the Baltic Sea area in the fall months. I was ready for the solitude of the sea coast.

It was a crisp October morning when we arrived in Putlos. The atmospheric conditions were just right for us, and we began our firing practice on the second day. We were so busy in the beautiful weather that I feared I would have no time to myself. By the sixth day, however, the fall rains came and firing practice was discontinued for more than a week.

The rains meant we would have to stay longer in Putlos in order to complete the firing, so I was the only man in the entire battalion who was glad to see the inclement weather.

Armed with a New Testament, one copy of the complete Bible, and two legal-size tablets, I found a private spot in one of the larger tents. I began to study and make notes, to read and to write.

I still had a slight tendency to find something of assurance in my initial experience with the Lord—plus the subconscious urge to "feel" saved. However, since John gives attention to neither of these factors, I endeavored to satisfy myself with an interpretive explanation of his vital signs of spiritual life.

It was the week that provided the impetus of my solid scriptural assurance that I am born again.

Though I came to complete peace about my own salvation in a matter of weeks (after studying the vital signs!), the months and years since that experience in Germany have provided me with fresh insights into this important subject.

Let's examine the spiritual vital signs closely. I hope my journey will be a help to yours as we look at those affirmations of assurance . . . making them ours.

FIVE
A LIFE STYLE
OF WILLING OBEDIENCE

The inundation of water which swept our seaside encampment provided me opportunity for study time. The northwest rains from the Baltic were of such overwhelming proportions that I likened them in my own mind to the monsoon rains of South Asia.

Virtually all military activity ceased because of the weather. Having found my private spot, I began my studies. The scene depicted the perfect setting for "curling up with a good book"—there were pelting rains and more than gentle winds surrounding my warm, dry study area. It would have been a psychologically "cozy" atmosphere except for one thing—I felt I was fighting for my spiritual life!

I had noted in my reading of 1 John a forceful statement in the last chapter of the book (5:13). John emphasizes that he is writing of these evidences of salvation in order that his readers will know whether they have eternal life. I had been observing that word "know" as I repeatedly read through the letter. I had marked its usage and was cognizant that it appears many times throughout the small epistle.

Yet, the depth of what I was reading had not occurred to me. In my confusion—under the emotional strain of wanting to "know for sure" about my salvation—I clouded my recognition and understanding of clear statements from Scripture. My spiritual dysfunction during that time caused me to read words without regard to their meaning and import. This is common among Christians who are doubting their spiritual birth. It is possible for us to read, then cloud the meaning of biblical truths with our doubts.

I had parroted that word "know" many times in my studies of John's book. I had underlined the word in my New Testament, but I had not allowed the simple intention of the writer to "come through" to me.

Finally, it did!

I came to the ecstatic conclusion that where John says we may "know" whether we have been born again, he means we *actually can know for sure!* No more guessing! No more hoping! No more "feeling"! I could *know!*

The conclusion immediately brought two thoughts to my mind.

First, my friends in the Thursday night Bible study were wrong! Genuine Christians sometimes *do* have confusion concerning whether they have been converted. This is why John has given so much of his book to the subject.

Second, though I still did not know if I actually had been born again, I was about to know definitely—one way or the other. If I was not saved at the time, I soon would be!

This was an even happier assumption!

I carefully worked through the book again, this time recording how often John uses the word "know." He employs it thirty-five times. I remember thinking to myself: "At least one of those 'knows' fits me!"

I have found they all do.

The first vital sign is mentioned in the second chapter, verse three. John utilizes brilliant redundancy as he sketches his first proof of conversion: "We know that we have come to know Him."

It is imperative that you rid yourself of any thinking which will disregard the meaning of the words you read or hear. John says we may know with certainty that we are saved—or that we are lost. You must allow his words —in all of their reality—to penetrate your mind.

It is the only way you will find assurance.

Where Scripture indicates that we can "know" that we "know Christ," it means concisely and precisely that! You must accept the fact that the Heavenly Father wants you to have complete assurance that you have been born again.

The word which John uses for "knowing" has the connotation of knowing something by observance—a first-hand *experiential knowledge*. It is a sure knowledge, predicated upon what we observe or experience for ourselves. The simple, mundane comparison between "book learning" and "practical experience" fits here. John speaks of practical experience.

There is that word "experience" again. You have noted how adamantly I am opposed to basing our assurance on just one experience, even the experience of conversion. Here is a good reason: We will possess a more certain grasp of our salvation with these daily, up-to-date, current experiences of *knowing*.

This knowledge of salvation is gained in the laboratory of life. It is not arrived at by snap judgment or hurried conclusions. It is posited on daily observance of the spiritual vital signs. "We know by our experiential knowledge." In this instance, it is a knowledge gained by our obedience to Christ, or in John's words, "keeping his commandments."

It takes some time and thought to gain this permanent assurance of salvation. You have already attempted to settle the matter by reading a pamphlet or a tract; you have taken someone's advice about a Scripture text, or listened to a sermon on "How to Know If You Have Been Born Again." None of these provided you with any permanency of conviction about your personal salvation. "Instant assurance" for a doubter seems never to last.

Now we are coming to investigate what God's Word says about the matter. He knows how to give us lasting assurance. Remember, this is a "journey," not a brief dash. Let's keep looking at the vital signs... unhurried.

If you do, it will become more and more *your* journey....

The first vital sign has to do with *a life style of obedience.*

Since we can know for sure about our salvation, let's look at the vital sign in its entirety: "By this we know that we have come to know Him, if we keep His commandments" (2:3).

John's terse statement makes us aware that Christians are serious concerning their obedience to the Lord Jesus. Our daily experiences of being obedient to the Lord Christ give us laboratory, *experiential* knowledge that we have been born again. This obedience to Christ and his teachings is the "fruit," the result of our new birth. We can look back over our lives in the past—and our commitment to Christ in the present—and we can know by our "life style of obedience" whether we in fact have been converted to him.

John does not refer back to the new birth itself for assurance, but to the life of obedience that the spiritual birth produces—not just to the "one" experience, but to the *many* experiences which have grown out of the initial one.

So, our daily experiences of obedience to Christ make us know that we have been born again. But... do not come to any hasty conclusions. Let's keep turning this diamond of truth, viewing some of its other facets.

When that stringent expression of the first vital sign roared its way into my understanding it set me back several weeks in my pilgrimage. *"Keep his commandments!"* Remember, I was not at my mental or emotional best during those days. Though I was aware that perfection is not demanded from Christians, I knew how serious John is about our obedience to the Savior. I recall my youthful discomfiture: "Who *is* able to obey him every time?"

Adding to my mental dishevelment was the fact that I had thoroughly consumed the first chapter of 1 John. We are clearly told there that if we claim there is no sin in our lives (in the present!), we are deceiving ourselves. It is evident that John is speaking of Christians. *Christians* are guilty of disobedience, it seems, even after they are born again.

I felt I had been guilty of disobedience. Obviously, the "sin question" was one of the primary factors in the beginning when I doubted my salvation. I professed to be a Christian, yet there was sin in my life. John's remarks in the first chapter of the book were encouraging to me—that born-again people still sin. But his blunt, unvarnished disclaimer in chapter two initiated even more consternation: "The one who says, 'I have come to know Him,' and does not keep His commandments, is a liar, and the truth is not in him" (2:4).

My confusion was removed only after I came to the conclusion that there had to be a "balance" between those statements of John. There is a vast difference between the Christian who still sins and the unbeliever who refuses any attempt at obedience to the Lord. I was confident of discovering the "balance" because he promises us thirty-five times that we can "know."

I cannot put into words the thrill which had flooded my spirit just a few days earlier (while still at our home base of Wiesbaden), when it became clear to me that I could "know for sure" about my personal salvation. The many disappointments which had been mine concerning assurance "one way or the other" had led me to think I was one of those people who would *never* possess certainty about the matter.

I set out to reconcile the two thoughts which were divergent concepts in my mind. I wrote on one of those legal-size tablets: (A) Those who refuse to obey Christ are not saved, even though they may claim to know him. (B) Those who are saved still have sin in their lives, but they do know Christ as Savior.

Slowly, without realizing I was "interpreting" the New Testament, I began placing Scripture against Scripture, verse alongside verse, in an attempt to understand John. Although I had the two concepts in mind, I still had not fully realized—according to the vital sign—what placed a person in one of the two categories, the "lost" or the "saved."

One of the early questions a person usually has is: If both the Christian and the unbeliever sin, how much sin makes a person "lost," and how little sin allows one to be ranked among the "saved"? I sought an answer to that and other questions. I literally lived in the New Testament for several days, there in our Baltic camp. I was comparing Scriptures, confident of John's thirty-five "knows."

I *knew* I could *know!*

The term which began to offer satisfaction to my thinking was "willing obedience." Since our wills must be exercised in following Christ, "willing" obedience seemed to be the key to keeping his commandments. It has to do with attitude, with life style.

Having come to the satisfying term of "willing obedience," I was forced to do some searching within—concerning my own "willingness." Though I did not spend a lengthy period of time in the search, I did not come to a "rushed" decision.

I had to work through a maze of inner rebuttals before I came to what I considered an honest conviction that I was willing to do anything the Lord wanted of me. I put myself through an overbearing self-analysis. What I called "total honesty" was nothing more than hyper-self-criticism; what I termed complete "personal integrity" was actually self-deprecation. These are obstacles one must face when conducting a non-professional self-analysis.

I had been guilty of disobedience to the Lord. Sometimes it was due to personal weaknesses; often it was the result of simple ignorance; occasionally it was precipitated by the spirit of plain rebellion. I came to know, however, that deep within me there was a spirit of willingness to obey fully the Lord Jesus.

Having worked through the obstacles, I came to the "conscious comprehension" that I possessed an attitude of willing obedience to our Lord—both to his written commandments and to his personal Spirit-impressions.

The "willingness" was representative of my true life style.

I made notations on the legal-size tablet. In the upper left corner of the page I wrote: "Not perfect, but saved." In the upper right corner I scribed: "Not obedient, and lost." I drew a line from each of those corners to the center of the page where I penned: "The difference between these two corners is willing obedience." I underlined the word "willing."

John maintains we can *know* that we know Christ—if we keep his commandments. Admittedly, we do sin; *however*, if there is an attitude about us which makes us willing to obey him, it is positive evidence that we know Christ, that we have been born again.

How pleased I was to say with confidence that I was willing to obey the Lord Jesus!

It is vital to note that the attitude of "willingness" to obey must be present within us before there will be consistent, specific *acts* of obedience to the Son of God. We shall come to the specificities of obedience shortly, but before we do, let's turn the diamond of truth once more and look at still another facet of willing obedience.

The whole issue of the first vital sign is "obedience," keeping Christ's commandments. The matter of willingness, of attitude, is the very foundation of obedience to him. Please allow me to be slightly technical for a brief space. I want to illustrate the "willing obedience" attitude with the use of the word "keep" which John uses in the vital sign.

In the phrase, "keep his commandments," the little word "keep" is from a Greek word which means to guard, as a soldier keeps guard over an assigned area. I mention three other uses of it in the New Testament that will shed interpretive meaning upon John's use of it.

In one instance, the word denotes the Jews' "keeping" of the Sabbath (John 9:16). It is true that by New Testament times much error had entered into the Sabbath observance; but it is a fact that the Jews practiced a rigid adherence to it. No pious Jew would have even *thought* of deliberately trampling underfoot the Sabbath, for any reason. It was settled one-time-for-all-time in the mind of the Jew to observe the Sabbath.

Many Christians have that same conviction about Sundays. Long ago they decided that the Lord's Day would belong singularly to him.

John feels the same way about all the body of commandments.

The attitude of the Christian toward obeying "all" the commandments of our Lord should be as intense as that of the Jew in keeping this one commandment!

We are not to "sort out" and discard those commandments which seem to demand too much from us. The Lord Jesus—in our new birth—does something to our hearts that makes us desire to be all that God wants us to be. In the Christian's heart, there is a settled principle of obedience to everything God demands. This is one attitude about keeping *his* commandments.

The second use of that word "keep"—the same one John uses in the vital sign—is in Acts 16:23. After Paul and Silas had been arrested in Philippi and placed in prison, the jailor was given explicit instructions to "keep them."

The jailor did two things which graphically reflect his understanding of the gravity of "keeping" those prisoners. He forced them into an interior cell, securing their feet in stocks. After the earthquake, when he thought they had escaped, he was ready to fall on his sword in suicide. He would rather have died than face those Roman authorities with the confession that he had "failed to keep" his prisoners.

Again, it should be in the heart of all Christians that we would rather die than face our Lord with the admission that we had "consciously" and "willfully" failed to keep even the least of his commandments!

I share a third way this word "keep" is employed in the New Testament. In 1 Corinthians 7:37 Paul uses the word as he describes the importance of keeping the moral purity of a maiden so she will be presented as a chaste virgin to her husband upon marriage.

What a sober responsibility rests upon us as parents! It whiplashes my soul even to think of one of my daughters losing her purity. I would be willing to die to preserve them morally. I am intent, watchful, anxious about their young lives. I am sure most parents feel the same.

Now, this same intensity, watchfulness, anxiety which most parents would feel about preserving the moral purity of a daughter . . . the Christian should be "seething" with this same vigilance concerning the "keeping" of the commandments of the Lord!

We admit that often the Jew did violate the Sabbath, the jailor did fail to keep the prisoners, and some parents have failed to keep the moral purity of their daughters —but it was not in their hearts to fail.

This same attitude is a part of every person who has been born again—an attitude of willing obedience. Often we fail in following our Lord, but it is not in our hearts to do so!

Before you come to a conclusion about yourself that is both premature and negative, please continue the journey. I have no desire to give you even the slightest assurance that you are a Christian if you have *not* been born again; however, I want you to walk through all that John says to us before you emotionally deadlock yourself out of the kingdom of our God and his Christ!

You may have already decided that you do not possess such intensity of obedience to the Lord Jesus as illustrated in the Jew, the jailor, and the parents. But are you *willing* to be that obedient to God? If you are willing to develop such an attitude of obedience in your life, it is an indication you have been born again.

It is a part of the vital sign; you know by your attitude toward the commands of Christ whether you are willing.

I found these scriptural illustrations in the New Testament years after my period of doubting. Although my assurance had been on "sound footing" for a long time when I discovered the illustrations, it startled me to read of such severe expressions of obedience. I could not honestly say, at the very moment I discovered the illustrations, that I was willing to follow Christ in that kind of commitment. There was one thing I did know: I was *willing* to be willing!

There is room in our Christian pilgrimage for growth in commitment—when we are willing.

We have given much attention to the principle of "willing obedience" to the Lord Jesus. There is a reason we have given so much space to the broad, general concept of obedience as a life style. It is important that we grasp the life principle of this vital sign of "commandment keeping." John is not writing to us about embracing a system of ethics, a code of morality or a standard of behavior. He is attempting to make us realize that *our attitude of obedience to the lordship of Jesus* is evidence that we have experienced the new birth in the past!

Now, let's look at this vital sign of "commandment keeping" in a more specific manner. The broad, general life principle of obedience to the Son of God has many tangibles, many acts of compliance.

The commands to which John alludes include the whole body of Scripture. *Our willingness to obey the Lord Jesus includes his negative commandments.*

Many things are clearly delineated in Scripture in the negative sense—the relative injunctions of the Old Testament; the prohibitions in the letters of Paul; the restraints mentioned by James; the forebodings of the book of Acts; even the restrictions in the teachings of our Lord. These are usually specific, detailed, clearly outlined.

There is a tendency on the part of many of us to think of his negative commandments in terms of the violent, the dastardly, the dreadful, the appalling. The Bible well condemns degeneracy, in unequivocal terms. The "gross" sins referred to in Scripture are repugnant to most people—even to unbelievers.

It is not necessarily a vital sign of conversion that one has refrained from drunkenness, adultery, theft, homicide, embezzlement, etc. Commendable as it is for us to abstain from such sins, many non-Christians practice similar abstinence.

There are other negative commandments which, measured against the standards of our existing culture, may seem of relative unimportance. Their importance, however, lies in the fact that they represent the will of God for the Christian believer.

There are many biblical injunctions and ordinances which guide the follower of Christ in the "negative" sense, and a careful response to this guidance often is referred to as "legalism"—a code of "legalistic" *do's* and *don'ts*. The great difference, however, between "legalism" and "simple obedience" is the Christian's commitment to the lordship of Christ—even to his negative commands!

By this we know that we know Christ, if we keep his commandments—*even his negative ones!*

Those who have been born again do not find these negatives of the Word grating; they delight in them. Obviously, we grow in our understanding of biblical truths, and at times we temporarily recoil from some specific teaching. But we do delight in the law of the Lord; it is our nature to so do.

The truly born again saint is more likely to be relieved than rebellious at the loving teaching of our Heavenly Father.

Though we have presented the negative aspect of obedience, the positive corollary is of equal importance. Some professing Christians tend to explain their obedience in terms of things they "do not do." The Word makes it clear to us, however, that following Christ in salvation means *obeying his positive commandments also.*

There are many, many things we are commanded to *do*, and this is a part of the obedience John says will result from knowing him. Everything the Lord has in his heart for us, *we* have in our hearts. He has done something within to give us such deeply entrenched convictions. It is called "the new birth."

If we have such conviction about obeying him, our spiritual vital sign reads "life."

By this we know that we know Christ, if we keep his commandments—even his *positive* ones!

The Lord Jesus has orders for our lives that are in addition to what is written in Scripture—*his unwritten commandments.* These unwritten commands for us are never in opposition to the written Word—simply "in addition to" the sacred writings.

Every Christian has these unwritten commandments from the Lord. Some of them are common to every saint; some are unique to a particular believer. There are areas of discipleship Christ has for my life that are different from yours, and you have direction from the Lord that he has given to no other person.

The unwritten commands come to us in particular applications of a scriptural principle, from God's providential will in our lives, and from impressions received of the Holy Spirit.

Our willingness to obey these unwritten commandments of the Lord is indicative of his life within us.

Again, by this we know whether we know Christ, if we keep his commandments—*even his unwritten ones!*

There are commandments from our Lord which are yet in the future. This aspect of his lordship I understood while still in the "Baltic School" in Germany. I realized that he was to have control over the rest of my life. Then, in my youth, there were many yet-to-come commandments from the Lord Jesus; today, in my maturity, there are still many yet-to-come commandments.

If we are willing for him to be Lord in every area, for all time, then our vital sign registers "life."

Or, to put it another way . . . by this we know that we know Christ, if we are willing to keep his commandments—*even his yet-to-come ones!*

We have turned this diamond of truth over and over to view it from as many perspectives as possible. It is time for you to be looking—still without haste—toward the completion of this journey into assurance.

Stare right into the face of this biblical truth: if your life style is one of willing obedience to the Son of God, mark it down, you have been born again! You are saved!

Still, when attempting to find complete assurance of salvation, we are wise to look at all of the life signs. The next step of our journey has to do with the Holy Spirit living in us.

It continued to rain viciously during those days on the Baltic, but little by little, the sun was shining through to me.

I felt a "breakthrough" was in sight.

This much I knew: I was *willing* to be obedient to the Lord Jesus. . . .

SIX
THE HOLY SPIRIT WITHIN US

I was not the only soldier who took advantage of the rains to embark on his own private venture. No one was doing anything pertaining to the military except taking meals in the mess tent. Some of the men read, many of them gambled, a few simply engaged in army type "bull sessions." They referred to my semi-private corner of the tent as the "chaplain's office."

After more than a week of such inactivity, our captain called us into the mess tent one afternoon just prior to the evening meal. He informed us that we were going to receive a break from doing "absolutely nothing." He then offered us trucks for transportation into the nearby town of Todendorf for a night's entertainment. A night's entertainment for most of our personnel meant frequenting the bars in the little town.

The captain warned that drivers of the vehicles would not be allowed to drink, since the roads were narrow and winding, and the weather treacherous for travel. Knowing that everyone who made the trip would be drinking, I laughingly asked him who would be watching the drivers to insure their abstinence. The captain laughed with me, then retorted, "Reynolds, you don't drink! *You* can drive one of the trucks! Surely you won't mind us getting you away from your private monastery for just one evening."

The men cheered.

Those who were safety conscious asked to "ride with Reynolds."

I drove a truck to Todendorf.

It was after 8:00 p.m. when we arrived in town, and the rains were again torrential. I parked in a well-lighted area of the business district and settled down to sleep in the seat of the cab. The heavy rains forced me to keep the windows closed, and the closed windows made the cab too hot for napping.

Unable to sleep, I decided to spend my time memorizing all of the spiritual vital signs in 1 John. I had already made the five categories we are using in this book.

I did not have light enough to read comfortably, so I would glance at the vital signs I had marked in red, then repeat them over and over in my mind. The one which speaks of the Holy Spirit living within us captured my attention: "By this we know that we abide in Him and He in us, because He has given us of His Spirit" (4:13).

That night, for the first time during my period of doubting, I seriously questioned whether the Spirit of God lived within me. I had begun to be comfortable with the vital sign of obedience, but now I wondered how I could know if the Spirit lived inside me.

I admit the rest of the evening was a very unhappy experience for me. I waited restlessly until well after midnight for all of my riders to return to the truck. The last two hours were spent wondering anxiously how I would be able to "know for sure" whether the Holy Spirit lived within me.

While driving back to the encampment near Putlos, it came to my mind once more that John tells us thirty-five times we can "know" about our personal salvation.

It was good to remember.

I could know!

I laughed happily to myself.

The next morning I began looking earnestly at the vital sign of the Spirit's presence in us. Since I did not have a thorough grasp of the New Testament as a whole, I stayed with the information John gives us about the Holy Spirit residing in the Christian. He tells us twice that we can "know" we are in Christ, and Christ in us, by the Spirit he has given to us (3:24; 4:13).

The word which John uses for "know" in this vital sign is the same one he employs for the vital sign of obedience. It is a knowledge which comes from practical experience. We can know from our own observance if the Holy Spirit actually lives in us. Though I knew nothing then about the Greek word, I did accept what the English versions assert: We can "know" he lives in us by the Spirit whom he has given to us.

How then *could* I know that the Holy Spirit lived in me?

One of the evidences surfaced quickly. It took only a brief period of time for me to retrace mentally the Spirit's convicting work in my life. Incident after incident came to my mind. I vividly recalled times when he had "arrested me" in an almost physical way because of some sinful act or attitude. He *does* know how to get our attention when we are disobedient!

John says we can know by observance. I had made many observations about the Spirit's convicting work in me. I understood about that word "conviction" even then. I did not know where it was in the New Testament, but I knew what the word meant in relation to the Spirit of God. All Baptists know that word "conviction" from infancy. We hear it a lot! We believe in it!

My most recent bout with the Spirit's conviction was the apex of my uneasiness concerning his presence in me. This is the reason I shared with you about the evening in Todendorf.

I engaged in some frivolous talk with the men in my battalion about their night on the town. Make no mistake, the men went into Todendorf to imbibe alcohol and to find "ladies of the evening." I had known and loved some of those fellows since high school days, and our unit had a great spirit of camaraderie, of *esprit de corps.* I did not want to cause any schism within our ranks of fellowship. In my attempt to make them know I was not condemning *them* as persons, I made it appear that I condoned their actions!

Two days after the Todendorf trip, the skies cleared and we immediately resumed firing practice. The renewed activity put me into close contact with most of the men. The conversations in every quarter centered on the "night in Todendorf." It was important to me to be accepted among the men, and I laughed and jested with them about some terrible sins.

Such an attitude of lightness on my part with regard to their sin must have deeply grieved the Spirit of God who lives inside me. I am sure I did not sense his grief early in the day because I was so thoroughly enjoying the fellowship of the men. The trip to Todendorf, and my ensuing attitude, had made a difference with them.

Later in the day I came to be ashamed of my newly found acceptance with them. Late in the afternoon a fellow soldier placed his hand on my shoulder during one of those foolish conversations, announcing to the others, "This man Reynolds is a *real* Christian! He knows exactly what I was into the other night and hasn't said a thing about it!" The others laughed. They agreed I was a *real* Christian, not a hypocrite.

It was a dagger thrust into my heart. It was one of those "arrests" of the Spirit of God! I knew I had dishonored the name of Jesus, and had injuriously affected my own testimony. It was not that I had failed to speak about the matter to the man—the disappointment lay in the fact that he felt comfortable laughing about his sin with one who was a believer in Christ!

I was distressingly addled.

I spent the early part of the evening alone, walking the wet beaches of the Baltic.

That night I decided the Spirit of God probably *did* live in me. No one else could bring such pungent conviction into my life! No mere "conscience" could do what he did that day!

If, in fact, he lived in me, the vital sign would indicate that I was a Christian—I had been born again. But wait! I still was determined to look further into the matter. I wanted to know *from Scripture* how to be sure the Spirit lived within me. I had suffered through too many abortive assurances in the past months; I would not hurry myself.

I did not know it that night in Putlos, but I had discovered what I now call the "negative assurance" of the Holy Spirit.

I was glad to be closer to assurance of my salvation, though it was a *bittersweet* gladness. I thought I had identified the Holy Spirit within me, *but the recognition came because of a serious sin in my life*—that of engaging in light-hearted banter about some very deep sins!

I still intended to learn what Scripture said about the Spirit living within us.

Let's look closely at the scriptural interpretation of the vital sign. John tells us we can know we are in Christ, and Christ in us, by the Spirit whom he has given to us (3:24; 4:13). We may have objective verification of our salvation through the testimony of the indwelling Holy Spirit.

There is a statement in 1 Corinthians 6:17 which indicates that in the born-again person the Spirit of God and the human spirit become "one." *God's Spirit* and the *human spirit* are so inextricably bound together that they are in essence "one Spirit." *The Living Bible* translates the verse: "If you give yourself to the Lord, you and Christ are joined together as one person."

This is much more than the two spirits agreeing together, or being in harmony with each other; it means the human spirit and the Spirit of Christ are, in principle, one *Person!*

The Spirit of God has many vital functions which are a part of his intimate proximity to the believer. He is to guard, guide, comfort, illuminate, sanctify, rebuke, restrain. He makes the Lord Jesus personally "real" to us. Underlying all that he does in us, *he makes us know we are a part of the family of God!* This is why Paul refers to him as the "Spirit of adoption."

It is true that he is to empower us, but he also lives within to *support* us. It is a part of his "assuring ministry." Romans 8:16 tells us: "The Spirit Himself bears witness with our spirit that we are the children of God."

The Holy Spirit tells our human spirit that we belong to Jesus! This inner testimony of the Spirit of God has both a positive and a negative aspect.

When we are sensitive to the lordship and leadership of the Holy Spirit in our lives, *the "assurance factor" is quite positive.*

"Inner peace" is one of the by-products of obedience to the Lord. There is a peace which only the Holy Spirit is able to give us. It is that peace which passes all human ability to understand. It transcends intellectual perception. It is unaffected by any circumstances—physical problems, grief, financial perplexities, etc. None of these are able to rob us of the inner peace which is ours when our fellowship with the Holy Spirit is unimpaired by sin.

"Inner joy" is ours when we are obediently alert to the Spirit's presence within us. Sometimes the joy expresses itself externally, and we are on "cloud nine." More often, however, the joy is well below the surface, too deep to be affected by things external. The richness of this joy is such that it cannot be described with mere words: It is a joy *unspeakable,* filled with glory!

While the external aspect of this joy varies in its intensity, the internal aspect of it is quite stable. Our response to the Spirit brings a happiness, a mirth, which is a positive sign of his presence in us—of our own spiritual life!

It is true that joy and peace are emotions, but in the Christian they are not "unattended" emotions; they are "Spirit-attended" emotions. The deeply imbedded peace and joy in the believer's life are from the Spirit of God, expressed *through* the emotions. The emotions are *vehicles* of the Spirit's joy and peace—not the *source* of them!

Remember, the Christian's spirit and the Lord's Spirit are joined as "one Spirit." What affects one affects the other. When we are sensitive and obedient to the Lord, it brings joy to the Spirit of God. Because our spirits are so bound up in his, when he is joyful, so are we! Our joy and our peace come from him!

Just hours before he went to the cross, the Lord Jesus said, "My peace and my joy" I give unto you. The Spirit of the Lord Jesus still dispenses that peace and that joy to born-again persons. He distributes them from the "inside," and he lives only on the inside of Christians.

If *he* gives you peace and joy when you are obedient, it is an evidence that he lives in you . . . and that is proof that you have been saved!

In our journey we are attempting to leave "no stone unturned," and no facet of assurance overlooked. We shall now consider another perspective of the Spirit's assurance to us—*his negative assurance.*

When we live with an acute awareness of the claims of Christ on our lives, the joy of the Holy Spirit permeates every part of our being. We are contented, happy, at peace with God, at peace with ourselves.

But when we are disobedient—no matter how temporarily so—we are unsettled, unpeaceful, unhappy.

This is *the negative assurance factor of the Holy Spirit.*

While nothing can destroy our *relationship* with the Spirit of God, a sinful thought is detrimental to our *fellowship* with him. He is a Person, and he can be grieved (Eph. 4:30). Since he lives within those of us who are saved—when he is grieved, so are we!

We who have been born again cannot live sinfully and be happy with ourselves. Our spirits will be grieved by the Holy Spirit who lives in us.

Interestingly enough, the fact that we are unhappy when we are disobedient to Christ is a concrete evidence that we are born again. It means the Holy Spirit lives within us. His living within us means we have been converted to Christ!

The Living Bible translates the vital sign: "He has put his own Holy Spirit into our hearts as a proof to us that we are living with him and he with us" (4:13).

Please allow me another "flash forward" to illustrate this negative assurance of the Spirit.

Some years ago I was invited to deliver a series of special messages on "assurance of salvation" to a Christian college in the South. The last message of the series concerned itself with the negative assurance of the Holy Spirit. I lightly referred to it during the message as "assurance in reverse."

The college librarian, knowing I had intended to leave the campus immediately following the chapel service, asked if I would take the time to come by her office. Tears of joy were streaming down her face as she admitted me into the room. She had come to a full assurance of her salvation during the chapel hour.

"For the last twenty years I have thought I probably was not truly a Christian—that I had not been converted," she confessed. "Today I have come to understand that what I thought was a sign of being unsaved is a sign I *am* saved!" *Fresh assurance!* She unfolded to me how, during those twenty years, every time she sinned she experienced an inner turmoil. She interpreted the raging within to mean that she had not been born again.

I employed my favorite expression for the Holy Spirit as I further explained "negative assurance" to her: "Resident Lord." I told her she would probably be appallingly sinful were it not for her resident Lord who "lives in"; that he made her so miserable when she wandered outside the will of God that she was compelled to return. Because she knew there was both lightness and exaggeration on my part, she readily agreed to my remarks.

As I stood up to leave her office, she enjoined me always to explain about that "assurance in reverse" when talking to doubters.

I always have.

Our unhappiness when we are disobedient to our Lord is evidence that the Spirit of God lives in us; his presence in us is evidence that we know Christ!

Negative assurance: A person who is living sinfully, who *knows* he is living sinfully, who *enjoys* living in such a manner, who intends to *continue* that sinful way of living—that person does not have the Holy Spirit living within him. The very fact that he is "comfortable" about his sin is proof of the Spirit's absence.

His spiritual vital sign registers "no life."

But for those of us who cannot be happy in our sin, the Spirit of God lives in us; we have proof of the life of God within us. We are saved!

I noticed—while still on the Baltic—that some of the peace and joy of the Holy Spirit were coming back into my life. They were returning almost imperceptibly, not with any dramatic flourish. It was good for me. I was beginning to practice his presence.

Though it was difficult for me at times, I did not allow myself to hurry into complete assurance. I wanted a stable kind of certainty. I never wanted to go through such doubting again.

Let's take in every step of our journey into assurance. It will be better for us in the end.

SEVEN
LOVING OTHER CHRISTIANS

The firing practice was completed just a few days after the rains subsided, and we broke camp to head back to our home base in Wiesbaden. While we were on the Baltic I gave scant attention to the vital sign of "loving other Christians."

I had discovered the vital sign three months earlier, during the summer, and had considered it often during the days of July and August. During those two months, when I had a tendency to condemn myself, the verse in chapter three (3:14) would give me a bit of comfort. It says: "We know that we have passed out of death into life, because we love the brethren. He who does not love abides in death."

The verse was meaningful to me because it speaks with such precise clarity: "We have passed out of death into life." I liked that clarity! I could understand that. Another reason I was fond of the verse is that I thought I had loved other Christians in a special way. In particular, I had both great affinity and great patience with them. In short, the statement from John's pen encouraged me to believe I had been born again. This greatly aided my spirits during the summer.

The trip from Putlos to Wiesbaden encompassed three full days in an Army convoy of some forty vehicles. I rode with a friend named Jack Dunham who was from a southern state. Jack was an easy fellow with whom to talk, was from a Baptist background, and generally "wore well" around the other men.

We spent the first day discussing baseball's recently completed world series. The second day's conversation lulled a bit, and I began studying some of the notes I had compiled concerning the vital signs. Jack and I bunked in the same tent in Putlos, so he knew of the great attention I had given to my study while we were there.

He seemed interested in my observations—especially the concept of the vital signs; so I shared some of my "conclusions" with him. As I explained the vital signs, Jack responded to each one with his characteristic verbal agreement: "I'll buy that." After he had "bought" all of the vital signs, he rescinded some of his agreement concerning this one of loving other Christians.

I can still see him in my mind's eye as he pursed his lips in both a thoughtful and pugnacious vein, insisting, "There are *just several Christians* I know who are *impossible* to love!" I gently chided him about his attitude, but to no avail. "Do you really want to obey the Lord fully? Do you honestly want to obey all his commandments?" He maintained that he did. "Well," I continued, "one of his commandments is that we Christians *love one another!*"

I confess I made little headway with my friend. He continued to insist that he wanted to obey the Lord, but there were "just several people" ranked among the saints whom he could not love. The only accomplishment I made that day was to coerce him into admitting that there was inconsistency in his thinking.

Please do not think my motive is to malign an old Army friend—I have not even used his real name. I have shared our conversation with you because Jack's attitude is all too common. I have heard it expressed many times through the years. I am not judging Jack Dunham or others who have confessed a similar disdain for "just several people" whom they could not tolerate—let alone love.

It's true, we *do* have a wide assortment of people numbered among the saints. I've been in this "business" a long time, and as the carney men say, "I've seen 'em all!"

In the church you will find many, many types:

The swaggering religious demagogues; unstinting doctrinal bigots...

Sophisticates with their artificial manners who have tried and pried and stretched and tampered with the true purpose of the church in an attempt to make it nothing more than a congregational "cage of culture"; the unrefined, who have so little respect for the gospel's claim on the total person that they would let the church degenerate into a "dustbin" of culture...

The spiritually obese, and those who are guilty of an exquisite put-on...

The woefully ignorant, who make their part of the body of Christ seem to be half-miracle, half-mess...

Exploiters, whose attitude toward the church is an artificial endearment mingled with a patronizing contempt...

Some who follow the line of least "existence" with reference to serving Christ; who drop you like so many cultured cuff links when you talk about self-sacrifice; who treat the church of the living Lord as if it were an adult Disneyland...

Mindless opportunists; unabashed braggarts...

The spiritually impoverished, who look upon any rupture in the church fellowship as a "rousing adventure," rather than a debacle to sicken the lives of the saints...

The ultra-bright glamour group, whose daily lives are slapdash sequences of tawdry little episodes, instead of monumental holy experiences of following the risen Christ—whose spiritual halos are so tarnished they need to be touched up with moral paint...

Those who have brought the "Bourbonic Plague" to a formerly teetotaling church...

Some who have lapses of moral nerve; some who nurse their "position" in the church like a giant condor sitting resolutely on a cracked egg...

Members-in-good-standing who seem to miss the real gut-crunch of the gospel; who ignore the searing relevancy of midcentury events...

Hyperactivists showing no inclination toward an analysis of what is dynamic or valuable in the life of the church; those who would rather "steal the play" than serve as useful "supporting witnesses"...

Post-Victorian popoffs debating about the morality of organ transplants, the corollary problem of when death actually occurs, and the effects of birth-control—but who refuse to be bothered with taking a basket of food to a hungry widow...

Loafers "marching" to their jobs in the church organizations with all of the enthusiasm of a medieval saint striding into a leper colony...

Compromisers with an unswerving determination to conciliate, accommodate, and otherwise come to terms with the world about us....

You will find them all in the church!

Admittedly, this is a distorted caricature of a small segment of the church's populace; however, before you allow my remarks to arouse you to some foregone conclusions, I beg you to digest this one sentence: *Your attitude toward this group I have depicted reveals your own spiritual condition!*

Read the vital sign once more: "We know we have passed out of death and into life, because we love the brethren." This is the most positive, the most incisive statement of assurance in all of the New Testament. Perhaps the reason John words it so unequivocally is that he knows the church all too well. Anyone who is able to love *all* of that crowd has the new nature God gives to born-again persons! Unconverted human nature does not possess the capacity to love like that!

I must make two remarks to you about this "crowd" I have portrayed. First, it is an incontestable fact that this "crowd" represents a minority of Christians. Most Christians are easy to love; in fact, it is not difficult for a pagan to love most saints. The true Christian, however, will go beyond and love even the unlovable. This is one of Christianity's distinguishing hallmarks.

Second, it is true that some of the above mentioned persons—though in the church—are not genuine Christians. They have not been born again. But it is for the Lord himself to perform the "sifting judgment." As for us, we are to regard as *brothers* and *sisters* all who are a part of the visible congregation of the saints; and God gives us the grace to love them!

There are some interpreters of the New Testament who suggest that John has the whole human race in mind when he speaks of loving "the brethren." They propose that he means the brotherhood of mankind. It is not within the scope of my purpose to answer that proposal in this work. Suffice it to say that if John has the whole of humanity in his mind, then our fellow Christians are certainly included in his all-encompassing statement... and the saints must no less love one another!

As we have mentioned, it is not difficult to love God's choicest children. The absolute test is whether we love *all* of them. Love for other Christians is a simple—but dynamic—proof of spiritual life. If you love all of the church, even those "several people," it is evidence that you know the Lord personally. Only Christ himself is able to implant such a love within you!

Now, let's reinforce our thinking even more with a thorough investigation of the vital sign. It has some aspects which are not found in the other signs.

John introduces this vital sign in the same manner that he does the first two—with the words "we know." The word for "know" in this verse is from a different Greek word than the others, but it has the denotation of "absolute knowledge." Again, we may "know for sure" we have been born again—if we have a special love for fellow Christians.

Of all of the vital signs, the one most emphatically stated by John is this one. Consider the other two at which we have looked. He says if we have "willing obedience" we will be able to know that we personally *know Christ* (2:3). He asserts that we can know for sure that *Christ lives in us* when we possess the Holy Spirit within us (3:24; 4:13). He has his most convincing word of assurance, however, in this avowal that *we have already passed out of spiritual death and into spiritual life* (3:14).

The word "already" is not a part of the verse, but the sense of it is there. It is something that has "already" happened to those of us who have a special love for Christians. That which has "already" happened to us is the new birth. We have been born out of death and into life.

The new birth is not our "reward" for loving Christians; our ability to love other Christians is the *result* of our being born again!

This love which born-again ones have for each other is of the highest order. It is not simply love which exists between families and close friends, it is the very essence of the love which God has for us. It is the same love described in John 3:16.

There are some distinctive qualities to this God-kind-of-love. Let's examine some of those distinctives.

It is a selfless love.

It is a giving love.

It is not mere sentimental friendship. Though friendship is one of the symptoms, the love Christians have for each other is far deeper, richer than friendship. Christians do possess a "family type" of love for each other. Children of God who are complete strangers are able to sense this love for each other in a brief time after becoming acquainted. There is a kinship which born-again persons feel for other saints which we do not, *cannot* feel for non-Christians.

The love of which John writes is not a "self-generated" love. This reciprocal love we Christians possess is the love of Jesus Christ flowing through those of us in whom Christ lives! One may feel an obligation to express this kind of love, yet not be able to produce it from within. It comes from God's presence in the human heart!

Of course this love we direct toward each other can grow. It can be heightened, deepened, widened as we walk in the Lord—but it cannot be self-generated.

This is why it is called a vital *sign*—it reveals what is within.

Not only does this love have some distinctive qualities, it is a love which is *commanded* of us by our Lord. It seems strange, perhaps, that such a Spirit-originated love would be commanded of the human heart, but God has conditioned the heart to receive such a commandment.

Love *can* be commanded of those of us who have been born again. To us, his commandments are not grievous, not burdensome (1 John 5:3). When the Lord Jesus tells us to love one another, he is not attempting to coerce us into doing something we have no desire to do. Rather, he is inciting us to do something that is already in our hearts to do.

The command to love one another is a "pep rally" kind of commandment. Across the United States there are thousands of schools who hold "pep rallies" for their athletic teams before each game. The objective of those rallies is not to instill a desire into the athletes to win their contest. The players already have such a desire within themselves. The purpose of the rally is to motivate, to "fan the flame," to incite those athletes in a particular situation. It is to stir up that which is already within.

The external commandment to love one another is quite insufficient apart from the new nature God gives to the born-again person. John joins our Lord in commanding us to love one another. Chapters three and four of his small epistle abound with references to our loving one another, but he predicates his admonition upon our being children of God—having God's nature. It is a "pep rally" kind of motivation. Every person in whom Christ lives will respond to it.

It is worth noting that our love for the brethren is not always cascading at the highest level of intensity. Our humanness, our current spiritual condition, our various circumstances all have to do with the *intensity* of our love.

There is an ebb and flow in our experiences of life—between the extremes of ecstatic happiness and dismal disappointment. This shift does not dilute the quality of our love for other Christians, but it does affect our attention to that love—and our expression of it in any given moment.

During the summer months, when I first discovered this vital sign of "loving other Christians," I felt good about the implications of it because I thought I loved Christians. I did not dwell on it, but my consideration of it left me with the impression that it meant I had at least some spiritual qualities.

In October, after returning from Putlos to Wiesbaden, I gave attention to it in my in-depth study of the vital signs. I soon realized that the vital sign gave me a "good reading." I knew that I did not love unbelievers in the same way I loved Christians. There was something special about the love I sensed for fellow believers. I did not *intend* to love those non-Christians less—it just seemed to be in my nature to love Christians more!

In studying the vital sign and the related passages in chapters three and four of 1 John, I knew that I did love Christians in the way John says that born-again people will love one another.

In the first chapter of this "journey" I suggested I had not been able to recognize any fruit of conversion during the early years of my Christian life. With my now slowly developing peace of mind, I was beginning to understand that there *were* evidences of Christ's presence within me during those early years. The evidence was solid: *I consciously sought Christian friends!*

I did not choose "Christian" friends to prove to myself or anyone else that I was born again—it simply fit my personal life style. I was frankly uncomfortable in close association "socially" with unbelievers. I liked those "church people." As a youth, all of my close friends were actively linked to the life of a church.

John tells us—in the same paragraph where he shares the vital sign—that we are to love in *deed* and in *truth*, not in mere tongue and word (3:18). That's the way I loved fellow Christians! My vital sign registered "life"! He notes that everyone who "loves" is born of God and knows God (4:7). My vital sign still read "life."

I continued reading those verses I had underlined in 1 John. The apostle cogently declares that if we love one another *God lives in us* (4:12). John seemingly cannot move away from this grand theme. He writes a sentence or two about other matters, then informs us again that *God is love,* that we who live in a spirit of "love" live *in God;* that God lives *in us* (4:16).

My vital sign?
Life!

While the fear of being unsaved was no longer knife-edged, the complete sense of assurance was still absent. One would think that such confidence on my part concerning this vital sign of "loving other Christians" would have brought me to a permanently abiding peace.

Not yet.

There is a reason why my "full assurance" was missing. I did not realize then that the vital signs interact with each other; I did not know that if *one* of the signs registered "life" that all the others would give the same reading.

I knew I had passed the "test" of loving other Christians.

I knew the Holy Spirit lived in me.

I was satisfied with my willingness to obey Jesus as my personal Lord.

There was, however, a serious question in my mind as to whether my nature had been changed—whether I had God's nature within me.

I thought I had to know every single detail of every vital sign. While I felt confidence about some of the signs, I had not come to a conclusion about others. I had some pre-conceived, self-imposed barriers—my own ignorance was holding back my full assurance.

I was still giving attention to the other signs, though, and still holding tenaciously to the conviction that God wanted me to have assurance of my standing before him.

Full assurance was coming!

October in Wiesbaden was coming to an end . . . and so were my days of uncertainty.

EIGHT
RECOGNIZING OUR
NEW NATURE

From the time I had arranged the vital signs into the five categories, I winced every time I looked into the one which indicates the "new nature."

I decided John is the most unbending of all the New Testament writers. There were times when I simply *disliked* him! In one of our Youth for Christ rallies the evangelist's message was from the book of Amos. As he reported the stinging rebuke which the prophet directed toward his listeners, the speaker informed us that all of the minor prophets of the Old Testament era were extremely frank. I thought to myself, "John belongs in *that* crowd!"

John's straightforward, unswerving vital sign concerning our new nature is the powerful conclusion of a paragraph in chapter three: "No one who is born of God practices sin, because His seed abides in him; and he cannot sin, because he is born of God" (1 John 3:9).

I had heard of the term "new nature" long before I had discovered the vital signs in 1 John, and I am sure that is the remote reason why the term found its way into the naming of this particular sign.

There were, however, for me, two immediate sources

for the word "nature" at the time I was studying in 1 John. The first source was a common term at the time: "a bad seed." It was a reference to the undesirable traits some people seemed to have inherited from a parent. I was not conversant with all that the phrase implied, but I knew it was a reference to a person's "nature."

John uses that concept of "nature" in the vital sign. He informs us that God's "seed" is in the person who has been born again—the "seed" meaning God's own nature. I did not know it then, but the Greek word for "seed" is *sperm*. God's spiritual *sperm* is in the born-again person. No wonder the saints have God's own nature!

The second source of my concept of "new" or "divine" nature was from Scripture itself—through a friend. My friend suggested that "there is a verse somewhere in the New Testament" which indicates we take on the very nature of God when we are saved.

We had no concordance of the Bible, very little knowledge of Scripture itself—but a great amount of determination.

After an exhausting search, we found that verse. It is in what my friend excitedly called "Second Simon." He knew it was the book of 2 Peter; his excitement in finding the verse momentarily got the best of him. The statement from "Simon" Peter is that we who are born again are "partakers of the divine nature" (2 Peter 1:4).

It was penetratingly clear to me that the Christian has a new nature—a divine nature, God's nature. I was not sure I possessed that nature, and according to John, there are no exceptions—*all* born-again persons have God's "seed" in them.

My chief problem was that I kept comparing my pre-conversion nature with my spiritual condition the day I was born again. I could not see that great, sweeping changes had come over me when I was ten years of age.

I understood that the change in nature has to do with an attitude concerning sin, but I could not comprehend

RECOGNIZING OUR NEW NATURE

that change in the life of a ten-year-old youngster!

I kept looking back, trying to impose that immediate night-to-day, darkness-to-light transformation of my *external* life—with no gray areas for growth.

Our Army unit was assigned to the Wiesbaden Air Force Base, one of our major military installations in Europe. The size and importance of the air base meant that all of its facilities were excellent and spacious.

One of the facilities I frequented was the library. During that October season when the vital signs were coming together for me, I did some studying in the reference section of the library. My intention was to read further concerning the physical vital signs—for better knowledge of comparison with the spiritual ones.

For me, it turned into the discovery of a rich spiritual vein—a "mother lode." It ushered in the virtual conclusion of my investigation into the vital signs.

In reading about the physical vital signs, I came to the realization that while they certainly do indicate whether there is physical *life*, their more important function is to clearly reveal the status of one's physical *health*. A blood pressure reading of 190-over-120 would certainly be an indication of "life"—but it would more vitally reveal a signally dangerous *health* problem.

It did not come over me in one "mental swoop," but that realization was the impetus of my understanding the vital sign of possessing a "new nature."

For the first time I was able to grasp that I had been expecting my *spiritual* vital signs—especially this one concerning our new nature—to register "perfect health"! Now I was able to see that they could register "life" even though my spiritual *health* may have been in poor condition!

This was a spiritual breakthrough for me!

Without being cognizant of it, I had been looking back once more to my conversion experience; I attempted to envision my newly converted self as immediately dwelling in the brightest part of the kingdom of light. But now I was remembering that being "born" into the kingdom of God meant I was in the beginning simply a "babe" in Christ... and though I received a new nature at my spiritual birth, *that nature needed an enormous amount of development.*

I thought to myself, "Maybe I *do* have God's nature in me! Maybe I *do* know Christ! Maybe I *am* saved!" Just the prospect of it made me so happy that I did not care at the time that my spiritual health might be wretched. I wanted to "know for sure" I had life! I could work on improving my *health* after I gained assurance of my spiritual *life.*

I was abruptly reminded that a library is no place to discover joyful truths of Scripture. Just the *thought* that I could be genuinely saved made me giggle like a child. The refined and matronly librarian was a serious-minded German lady who had tempered other of my disturbing library conversations in past weeks. This time she reprimanded me in her broken, ungrammatical English, calling my military rank as if it were a surname: "Mister Sargeant, I told you once more, you not supposed to laugh or spik out in library!"

We had a good relationship since I was often in the library. With her reprimand, I gathered my materials to leave. Going past her desk, still "giddy" with the joy of my discovery, I blurted out to her: "I'm the child of a King!"

"Ja," she spat back, "someday you be president."

"I already have a higher rank than that," I retorted.

Though my assurance was not complete, I knew I was on my way!

God's nature in *me*—in *Gene Reynolds!*

It was wonderfully overwhelming!

Walking from the library to my barracks, I even decided that the Apostle John was probably a good fellow after all.

Let's look together at the highlights of this important passage of the vital sign—1 John 3:1-9.

The Williams' translation of the New Testament gives careful attention to the grammatical aspects of the Greek verbs in verse nine: "No one who is born of God makes a practice of sinning, because the God-given life-principle continues to live in him, and he cannot practice sinning, because he is born of God."

Williams translates "God's seed" as "the God-given life-principle"—a reference to the nature of God which is in the born-again person.

The key to the translation of the verse is found in the phrase, "makes a practice of sinning." The phrase speaks of a life style, a nature. God's own nature in us will not allow us to "make a practice of sinning." It would be living against our very nature; our true nature will win out! God's seed—his nature—continues to live in us who are born again, and we cannot continuously live in a sinful life style.

John maintains his incisive brevity—and his uncompromising bluntness—in this passage on the vital sign. He states with succinctness that whoever "practices sin is of the devil" (v. 8) . . . and that "no one who is born of God practices sin" (v. 9). Our true natures are revealed with reference to the sin question.

We who know Christ have his nature within us—but we still sin. The difference is:

Before our conversion we sinned out of willingness.

Since our conversion we sin out of weakness.

The Christian still sins—but *loathes* it.

The non-Christian sins—and *loves* it.

The difference is in each one's nature.

Note once more the interaction of the vital signs. This

one of the "new nature" touches every one of the others. It is a basic description of the change the Son of God makes when he comes to live within us. Notice the correlation with the first three of the vital signs we have discussed.

If the Holy Spirit lives in you, he has changed your nature. *You* have the nature of God!

If you have a special love for Christians, it is because God has changed your nature—you have *God's* nature.

If you are willfully obedient to the Lord Jesus, it is because God has transformed you in your new birth. You have God's *nature* within you!

And since you have God's nature in you, you have a desire to live in obedience to the will of God.

Here are four guidelines concerning this nature of God within you.

First, you should note that the word "repentance" does not appear in the book of 1 John. As I attempted to discern whether I possessed God's nature within me, I kept wondering if I had *repented.* Repentance is another of those words we Baptists have known from childhood. I had known all of my life that I could not enter the kingdom of God without repenting. I could not recall, though, that the word "repentance" was even in my thoughts the day I was saved. Now I was wondering, did I actually repent? Was it a *genuine* repentance? Did I repent *enough?*

I knew that if I could pinpoint the genuineness of my repentance, I could believe I possessed the new nature. In my study of this vital sign it dawned upon me one day that John does not employ the word "repentance"—not one time—in his whole epistle. It is obvious from what he does say that he knows we *must* be repentant. But he majors on the fruit, the evidence of repentance, rather than on the act.

If there is a desire within you to live in the very center of the will of God, in obedience to the Lord Jesus, it is because you have repented—you have God's life, God's *nature* in you!

Second, take a positive stance concerning this matter of your new nature. During my time of doubting, I postured myself in the negative sense concerning this vital sign. I attempted to prove to myself that I did *not* possess God's nature. My rationale was this: If I could not prove to myself that the new nature was absent, then it must be present in me. I did not plan to approach my study in such a manner, but my fear of finding false assurance steered me into that avenue of searching.

Please view yourself with more kindness than I did myself during those days of doubting. If you have been this far on the journey with us, and you are positive about the first three vital signs we have discussed, then be positive about this one of possessing God's nature.

Approach it this way: Make the positive assumption that you *do* possess the divine nature, and unless you can convince yourself—*from Scripture*—that you are *not* a "partaker of the divine nature," then consider that you *are!*

It is time for you to exercise some positive faith in your commitment to Christ! You are the only one who can do it for you!

Third, so what if you are not in the upper 10 percent of the kingdom spiritually! What if you *are* in poor spiritual health? *That's* not your problem at the present! You need actually to establish from Scripture whether you know Jesus Christ—if you possess spiritual life!

You will never substantially improve your spiritual health until you have solid, full assurance of your spiritual life.

Besides, you have the rest of your earthly life to build up your spiritual health. For right now, lay hold on assurance of "life"!

Fourth, remember that your life is like a "section" of land—640 acres. When you gave yourself to Jesus Christ

in salvation, you gave him the total acreage of your life
—the whole of it!

He now has the title deed to all of it.

But as you and the Lord walk together over the acreage of your life, often he will point out to you that you have reserved a few acres for yourself—some intentionally, some unintentionally. As he brings this to your attention, telling you they must be under his lordship, say that you are willing for him to have them.

It is your *nature* to feel this way.

When you gave yourself to Jesus in salvation, he gave you this kind of nature—God's nature. The new nature within you is an evidence, a vital sign that you have been born again!

As I studied the vital signs and approached my own assurance, I came to appreciate John's inspired epistle more than I would have ever dreamed. In his "unbending" attitude concerning the new nature, I finally came to see that it was the very heart of the assurance which I was seeking.

I walked about the air base for several days in amazement. It still seemed too good to be true, that I could possess the very nature of the holy God. But Scripture maintains it is true . . . and I was trying very, very hard to believe it!

I did not hurry myself too much. I wanted to come to grips with that one last vital sign.

NINE
CONFESSING
JESUS CHRIST AS LORD

Jerome Hansen is a slow-talking, quick-thinking West Texan, and my "singing buddy" from Army days. We enjoyed harmonizing the old-fashioned gospel favorites. Though we sang "quartet" songs, it was usually just the two of us singing. The other men would not often join us, claiming they did not wish to break the perfect blend of my "corn field" tenor and Jerome's "down home" bass.

Jerome and I worked together—he was a brilliant computer and radar technician. During the leisure time we enjoyed between the "red alerts," we did a lot of singing —loud, boisterous singing. The nonsensical aspect of it was entertaining to the fellows with whom we worked.

Those fellows in our work area feigned interest in our singing. They knew *On the Jericho Road* was our favorite song. It gave each of us opportunity to display our own particular expertise in singing up and down the scale.

In mock appreciation of our musical abilities, the other technicians would liven up dull afternoons by requesting us to sing "The Jericho Road." In those instances we hammed it up to the screeching extremes of our vocal ranges.

During those months in which I gave such intense attention to the spiritual vital signs, I began to notice something about the way Jerome sang one line of our favorite song—he worded it differently in public than he did in private.

The song has a phrase in it which encourages us to take our burdens to the Lord Jesus. In private, Jerome would sing it the way it is written: "Just take it to *Christ*." However, when we were around other people, he always sang that line with these words: "Just take it to *him*." The pattern never varied.

His reluctance to mention the name of Christ in public bothered me at the time. It still bothers me.

Please understand that I loved and admired Jerome Hansen (I have not used his real name). But his reluctance to mention the name of our Lord in the presence of others *haunts* me to this day.

Jerome's reluctance to "confess" Christ in song or conversation initiated a thorough study on my part of the vital sign which speaks of "confessing Jesus Christ as Lord."

When I first discovered this vital sign, it did not ignite any intensive self-searching within me as did the others. My narrow logic and simplistic understanding of confessing Christ provided me with a sheltered satisfaction. I had "confessed" Christ when I was ten years old!

On the other hand, even if the remaining vital signs gave indication that I had not been born again, I was willing to make a new, *genuine* public confession of Christ as my Lord.

I had already decided to make another profession of faith—if the Lord so directed. I would go to the Youth for Christ rally, where a public invitation was extended in every service. I would respond to the appeal *by walking the aisle; by going to the front; by presenting myself at the altar* to publicly acknowledge before the audience that Christ had come into my life.

I would do it unblushingly, unashamedly, unhesitatingly. I would do it without embarrassment.

After all, I had come from an evangelical background —the Southern Baptist Convention—and I was familiar with the public profession of faith.

I was soon to learn, however, that my understanding of what it means to publicly confess Christ was treacherously limited; the New Testament concept of confessing Christ is much more than a one-time, mechanical confession in a public service.

Much more.

In this vital sign of "confessing Christ," John again writes with that precise clarity: "Whoever confesses that Jesus is the Son of God, God abides in him, and he in God" (4:15). If we confess Jesus before others, it is an evidence that Christ lives in us: We are born again!

Note, it is not *what* we confess, but *whom* we confess.

Admittedly, I had thought of confessing our Lord in terms of the method we evangelicals employ, rather than in terms of the principle presented in the New Testament. As I studied other scriptural remarks concerning a public confession, I came to the realization that it is broader, deeper than I had ever imagined.

I had a New Testament which was presented to me when I first entered military service. I think it was a gift from the Gideons. It had a brief appendix in it which instructed the reader where to find information on a few given subjects. I do not recall if I looked under "assurance" or "confession," but I was directed to some choice Scripture verses concerning the principle of public confession.

Three of those New Testament passages greatly illuminate the concept of publicly confessing Christ.

The first one is found in Matthew 10:32, 33: "Every one therefore who shall confess Me before men, I will also confess him before My Father who is in heaven.

But whoever shall deny Me before men, I will also deny him before My Father who is in heaven."

My concept of the public confession was heightened after a thoughtful consideration of these words of our Lord. A dual perspective evolved from the study.

The word "men" which Jesus utilizes is a generic use of the term; it is a reference to *mankind*. Our Lord is alluding to the "public domain." He demands much more than a "profession of faith" in a church service. *He demands that from the time of our conversion we spend our lives confessing him as our personal Lord and Savior—and that in the public domain.*

There is another perspective I learned from these words of our Lord. When I initially began to realize that a one time confession of faith in the church is insufficient obedience to the Lord's command, I was tempted to believe we should discard altogether that method.

Then I came to understand that the broader concept of the public confession does not negate the "method" of confession within the church. The solid rationale behind the method is quite simple to explain: If a "convert" will not openly confess Christ within the household of faith, it is doubtful that same convert will openly confess Christ in the marketplace. The method is good; it encourages the believer toward what is often that believer's first act of obedience as a Christian.

The second of those "confession passages" which assist in interpreting John's vital sign is Mark 8:38. Here is more teaching from the lips of Jesus: "For whoever is ashamed of Me and My words in this adulterous and sinful generation, the Son of Man will also be ashamed of him when He comes in the glory of His Father with the holy angels."

My ingestion of these sober words from our Lord inflamed my spiritual imagination! It became penetratingly clear to me that we do not confess to being Christians. We confess a Person—Jesus Christ. Jesus employs the personal pronoun—*Me!* We confess—him, not merely that we are embracing the Christian religion.

The Lord's words in Matthew also include the personal pronoun, but it was not until I read Mark's account, about being ashamed of *him*, that the crushing strength of his pronouncement shattered my simple and naive concept. One may not actually *deny* Christ, as he says in Matthew, but if that person is *ashamed* of the Lord Jesus . . . Christ will be ashamed to claim that one as his own when he returns for his saints!

The third, and the most prominent of the "confession passages," is Romans 10:9, 10: "If you confess with your mouth Jesus as Lord, and believe in your heart that God raised Him from the dead, you shall be saved; for with the heart man believes, resulting in righteousness, and with the mouth he confesses, resulting in salvation."

The phrase a chaplain suggested to me concerning the twofold aspect of this verse is "two sides of the same coin." He explained the obvious, that a coin is not "heads" or "tails," but both heads and tails.

He did not explicitly state it to me, but I inferred from his remarks that we must not separate the *believing* from the *confessing.* What we believe and confess is *one* thing, not two. They are two aspects of the same response to Christ. Paul is emphasizing to us that "confessing" is as indispensable as "believing."

A confession of faith before others is a *public confession* of a *private commitment.* There simply is no room for "secret believers" in God's plan. Perhaps that is why we are sometimes referred to in the New Testament as "followers" of Christ.

These three sections of Scripture—two from the lips of our Lord, one from the pen of Paul—greatly aid our understanding of John's vital sign. It is: "Confessing Jesus Christ as Lord." There is no other way to confess Jesus. He *demands* to be Lord!

In my investigation of this vital sign, I forced myself to

remain stoic, calm, unemotional. I was determined to find assurance of my salvation apart from some emotional quake; however, the study of these "confession passages" broke the barriers behind which I had placed my emotions in protective custody.

All heaven broke loose within me!

The "key" was the statement Jesus makes about "whoever is *ashamed* of Me." Never, *never* have I been ashamed of my faith in Christ. The fact that I claimed Jesus as both Savior and Lord had never been an embarrassment to me. I had spoken his name many times in that near-pagan military setting—and I did it without blushing! I had claimed him as *my* Lord, publicly, in my daily life, in the marketplace, on a college campus, in the military service!

John's vital sign of confessing Christ, strengthened by the words of our Lord, had registered "life" for me!

My emotional outlet at the first was through joyous laughing—then through joyous weeping! Yes, I was beginning to "feel good" about my relationship to Jesus Christ.

As Romans 10:9 says, I had confessed him with my mouth; I had spoken of him in my daily life. The assurance was coming!

I believed in Christ as my Lord; I was willing to espouse him passionately, to place my commitment to him in the bottom of my heart, and to transform that commitment into my reason for living!

I wanted the entire flavor of my life to confess Christ!

It is impossible to convey to you the joy within me during those days when this truth was developing in my thinking. Perhaps if I share a bit of the background, you will grasp something of the great sense of relief which was mine.

I have already mentioned that I have never been reluctant to speak of the Lord Jesus in the presence of others. This was true of me even during my teenage years. When I began to have serious doubts about my salvation, I still wanted to share the Lord with my friends. But there was a nagging, foreboding feeling that I should not do it.

My foreboding feeling had nothing to do with my *desire* to share Christ; it had to do with the honor of the Lord himself. The recurring thought in my mind was that it would dishonor Christ if I went about confessing him to others, then later had to admit to them that I had not actually known him at the time. It was not my personal pride which I held at stake, but the honor of the Son of God!

Of course, most of the men in my battalion knew I was a professing Christian, and they respected my life. But that was far different from "expressing with my mouth" what Jesus meant to me.

I had determined not to say anything about my relationship with the Lord during those fall months, except to a few close friends, until I settled the matter of my own salvation. As I turned to Scripture besides 1 John, I often read in the Gospels. I found things about the Lord Jesus I wanted desperately to share with others ... but I felt literally gagged.

I was spiritually *choking!*

Then, when the truth of "confessing Christ" dawned upon me, I felt I had been unbound, unfettered, unstifled! The "holding back straps" had been broken.

I could once more freely talk about Christ!

I was enjoying a wonderful inner liberty; the floodgates of joy had been opened.

For the first time in months I could say, without even a subtle trace of fear: "*I am saved!*"

We need now to bring together all of the various facets we have investigated. Let's begin with this vital sign of confessing Christ.

Are you willing to confess Jesus Christ as personally

alive within your life? Are you willing to tell others that you know *him*—not merely that you are a Christian? Can you do it "naturally," without having to force yourself to mention his name? Are you willing to confess that Christ, and Christ alone, is your hope of salvation?

If your answer is a spontaneous "yes" to these questions, it is because you have the life of God within you. You cannot "force" yourself to talk about Christ on a continuous basis if he does not live within you. On the other hand, if he *does* live within you, you cannot help but speak of him. You will not be able to contain it!

Two important thoughts come to my mind to share with you about your confession of Christ to others.

First, if you have been doubting your salvation, you most likely have not been aggressive to speak of him to others. Nevertheless, even during your period of doubting your hesitation was not because you were ashamed to mention him; it was because you were in a state of spiritual confusion. As I have informed you, that is what happened to me.

Still, even in a time of doubting, the Spirit of God living in us initiates a desire to confess him. One part of an old gospel song has these words: "I said I wouldn't tell it to a living soul, how he brought salvation when he made me whole, *but I found I couldn't hide such a love as Jesus does impart!*"

He does something within us which compels us to speak of him.

Second, you may be one of those people who are naturally quiet, who have a reserved, introverted personality. You do not speak out very much among others—about anything. I am not suggesting that because you know Christ you will become an outgoing, gregarious personality; not at all.

Do not compare yourself with some talkative friend who speaks freely with others about everything. We are here referring to personality traits, not character traits.

Christ must be confessed by all types of personalities. As a matter of fact, I have the gnawing suspicion that when quieter people speak about the Lord Jesus they receive a better "hearing" than those of us who are ready to talk at the proverbial drop of a hat.

But—introverted or extroverted—those of us who know Christ in our lives will confess him. We cannot help but do it.

At least a part of the divine reasoning behind confessing Christ in the public domain is that others will learn what he has done in our lives—a testimony to the unconverted. Such a testimony will be hollow, unconvincing if it is prompted by mere "duty" or a sense of obligation on our part. It must come from the inner workings of God in our lives.

If you have such "inner workings" in your life—motivating you to share Christ with others—it is an evidence, *a vital sign*, that you have spiritual life!

You have been born again!

You know Jesus Christ within!

Your vital signs read life—*all* of them. Remember, if one of the signs indicates life, so will the other four. They work interrelatedly with each other. Since this one of confessing Christ openly reads "life" for you, view the other four:

The Spirit of God lives in you. His presence in you is an indication of life.

You are willing to be obedient to the lordship of Christ in your life. The vital sign registers "life."

You possess the new nature God gives to those who are born again—"life."

You have a special love for other Christians—"life"!

All of the vital signs read "life" for you.

Take God at his Word—you are saved!

Do you wonder how I am able to make such bold, positive statements to you now, after admonishing you to move slowly, deliberately toward your conclusions?

It is very simple. Though I make such bold statements of your assurance in the light of the vital signs of obedience, new nature, loving, possessing the Spirit, and confessing Christ—*you* know if these are in your life.

You know!

My boldness is from this perspective: If these spiritual values are in you, *Scripture* is bold to assert that you have the life of God within you!

It is of vital importance that you believe Scripture at this point—that you simply, in childlike faith, take God at his Word.

He says you are born again!

There is one salient thought which should be projected about my arriving at "full assurance." I did not come to my assurance in any *one experience*—but through a series of discoveries in God's Word. There were many such discoveries over the months of my journey into assurance. The last few were merely the joyous culmination of all the others.

Also, I did not study the vital signs "one at a time." I have highlighted them to you in chronological order— the order in which I came to an understanding of John's intent for each sign. The study of one vital sign invariably overlapped the study of two or three more, and often it included all of the other four.

The concept of the "interaction" of the vital signs I did not discover until some time after I had come to complete assurance.

There now remains a wonderful capstone for the end of our journey together into assurance.

It comes in our one last step together. . . .

TEN
THE LAST STEP—
CONFIDENCE IN GOD

In the first few weeks I was in Europe, I was privileged to meet an American missionary to the German people. Her name is Jean Waltz. We met at the Saturday night Youth for Christ rally in Wiesbaden. She was in Wiesbaden often in relation to her ministry, and on those occasions she attended the rallies on Saturday night.

I rarely spoke with Jean Waltz except to pass amenities, simply because I did not know her well. She was a very pleasant person, and those who did know her well spoke of her spiritual depth and insight.

A mutual friend of ours—one of the fellows who participated in the Thursday night Bible study—told her I was unsure of my salvation, and that the doubting process had taken its toll on me.

Upon my return from Putlos and the Baltic, Jean Waltz was in Wiesbaden on one of her visits. She sought me out at the Saturday night rally, asking to speak with me. We had two conversations, each one lasting for more than two hours. She did not offer me an "easy assurance," but she did take a positive approach with me.

I shared with her what I had learned of the vital signs, and how I was determined to apply them to myself—

objectively and severely. It was at this point that she uttered the phrase, "Gene, you will have to, somewhere along the way, let go and *let God!*"

I had no idea what she meant.

In the second of our conversations she admonished me with that same phrase at least ten times: "You will have to let go and *let God!*"

I was embarrassed to tell her I did not know what she meant by the phrase, but every time she repeated it this thought would run through my mind: "Let God do *what?*"

Her conclusive word to me was that she felt I was truly a born-again Christian—and that I was going through the deep waters of doubt because God had something great for my life, and Satan was attempting to keep me from it through doubt.

So far, Satan had been successful, but Jean Waltz' confidence in me—based on Scripture—served as a tremendous encouragement.

My conversations with this missionary came during the days when I was seriously studying the vital signs of "possessing a new nature" and "confessing Jesus Christ as Lord." It was a time when I was attempting to muster more faith, a greater faith, a more positive faith—a more *practical* faith. John's epistle contains an assertive remark: "This is the victory that has overcome the world—our faith" (5:4). I wanted that kind of faith!

As I continued to delve into those two vital signs, I was conscious that I must "let go and let God"—though I was not sure what it meant.

It was out of this consciousness of "letting go and letting God" that I came to realize I must have *confidence in the character of God.* My faith, no matter how "strong," could neither save me nor give me assurance—but *God* could! I could trust him.

Jean Waltz' words finally made sense to me.

No matter how well we understand the vital signs, learn by our observations, or know by our experiences—the last step of our journey into assurance must be confidence in the character of our personal God. He has told us in his Word how we may know that we have been born again. We can depend on the character of God. He *means* what he says; he *says* what he means.

In 1 John 5:9 the apostle tells us that if we receive the witness of men, the witness of God is greater. We have personal friends in whom we have unquestioned confidence. If they relate something to be factual, we "receive their witness." All of us know people like that, in whose character we place the utmost confidence. John intimates that if we have such confidence in human character, "how much more" should we receive the witness of God himself!

God says we are born again if the evidences of the vital signs are present in our lives. It is not for us to muster *enough* faith to believe it. We are to place our confidence in the Heavenly Father! *He* says I am saved. I believe *him!*

If you will come to the assurance you desire—and the assurance *God* desires for you—you must simply believe God. If the evidences represented by these vital signs are in your life, the Father says you are born again.

You can believe *him!*

Ultimately . . . it is not our faith, but the God in whom we place our faith.

In 1 John 5:13 the beloved apostle does some "summing up." He offers a rationale for the epistle with his usual terseness: "These things have I written to you who believe in the name of the Son of God, in order that you may know that you have eternal life."

In just twenty-seven words John carries us "full cycle" through the theme of his epistle of assurance. The verse has three compact thoughts.

He alludes to *our simple faith:* "You who believe in the

name of the Son of God." Though John has a grasp of the profound things of God, he unfailingly keeps the gospel clearly simple. He never moves, in all of his depth, from the simplicity of faith in the Lord Jesus.

Though his brief epistle plumbs the enormous depths of what God does in transforming the life of a believer, John never varies from the "simple faith" concept which is the hallmark of the fourth Gospel—which he also wrote.

It is essential as we take this journey into assurance that we be not removed from the simple message of the gospel. Though we have delved beneath the surface in our investigation of the vital signs, we are conscious that we are saved by placing our faith in Jesus Christ! It is *still* this simple: "As many as received Him, to them He gave the right to become children of God, even to those who believe in His name" (John 1:12).

The weighty matters of the gospel have to do with God's love for us, with the substitutionary death of the Lord Jesus on his cross, with the mighty resurrection of the Son of God, with the coming of the Holy Spirit to live in every Christian believer.

Our response to this wonderful salvation of God is a "faith response" to the Lord Jesus. John alludes to our simple faith as he refers to us as those who "believe in the name of the Son of God."

John also refers to *our sure signs* in 1 John 5:13: "These things I have written unto you." The "these things" probably include the whole of the epistle; however, the heart of the little letter *is* the vital signs.

He has written to us who have this simple faith in the Son of God. He wants us to know for sure whether this faith of ours is alive. He wants us to have "assurance" that our response to Christ has been a "saving response."

So with his able pen he describes five spiritual vital signs which reveal whether the Son of God lives in us. If he does, we are born again.

One last time . . .

If we are born again, Christ has done something in us which makes us willing to be obedient to him. We have *a life style of willing obedience.*

If we are born again, God has done something in us and to us that gives us a special quality of love for the saints—that of *loving other Christians.*

If we are born again, Jesus Christ has transformed us so radically that we are different persons. *We possess a new nature—God's nature!*

If we are born again, the Lord Jesus has come in the Person of the Holy Spirit to live in us. *We possess the Spirit of God!*

If we are born again, we cannot contain that fact within ourselves. *We confess Jesus Christ as Lord and Savior, with our mouths, and that in the "public domain."*

At the risk of being overly repetitive, I wanted to list once more all of the vital signs. They are the "these things" John has written to us. These five evidences are the result, not the cause, of our being converted to Christ.

They are "sure signs"!

The third thought which John weaves into 5:13 has to do with *our sound assurance.* He pointedly informs us that he has written these things "in order that you may know that you have eternal life." The words "in order that" translate a Greek grammatical form which indicates "purpose." The *purpose* of John's writing the epistle is that we may *know that we have eternal life!*

How very much God wants us to know that we are saved!

The word here translated "know" is different from the word which means to "know by experience." Here John refers to a mental knowledge—a knowledge unaffected by emotions or circumstances.

I "know" that 10 x 10 equals 100. It is mathematical fact, regardless of any circumstances. That mathematical fact is unchanging, even though I may approach it plagued by the problems of deteriorating physical health, mental duress, or emotional depression. It is a "cold fact." None of my experiences has influence on it. It is unchanging truth.

It is this kind of stable, unchanging truth John has in mind with his use of the word "know." We may possess that kind of certainty about our eternal salvation. If the evidences of the vital signs are in us, we *know*—absolutely, unchangingly—that we are born again! This certain knowledge of salvation is John's reason for writing to us.

What kind of arrogance would allow us to claim such confidence as this?

It is not arrogance.

It is not self-confidence.

It is confidence in the unchanging character of the unchanging God!

That means in all seasons, in all circumstances, I may *know* I have eternal life. When I am rejoicing in the very center of the will of God—or even when my spiritual health may not be "up to par"—I have "sure knowledge" of my salvation, of my eternal life!

I have responded to Jesus Christ in simple faith. The evidences outlined in John's epistle are sure signs within my life. Based on God's Word and God's character, I have a sound assurance.

It is now time for *you* to gather all of the facets of this wonderful truth together, and quietly lay your confidence for salvation at the very heart of our unchanging, faithful God.

When you exercise that kind of faith in *him*, you will know that you have eternal life.

Then you will have full assurance.

During our Christian pilgrimage, we cannot live on the mountaintop continuously. Our common sense tells us this is true, as do illustrations from Scripture. There is *one exception:* We may take up permanent, uninterrupted residence on the "Mountaintop of Assurance."

After living in the Valley of Doubt for a few months, I wanted to be on the "peak" of that mountain for the rest of my pilgrimage—and I have been thus far! I know this is where God wants us to be.

There are so many treacherous valleys through which we must pass in this life, it seems imperative that we approach them from the Mountaintop of Assurance.

This is the only way of complete victory over those inescapable valleys.

I hope you will "let go and let God"!

Just a few years ago, I spent three hours in the international airport in Frankfurt, Germany. It was a fuel stopover between the Middle East and the United States. Wandering around the airport, my thoughts turned to Wiesbaden, just thirty miles to the south. I wished that there had been time enough to visit the lovely city, because of so many memories I possess from my time there.

I was returning from a visit to the Holy Land.

I recall thinking that two great cities of the world had influenced the invigoration and stimulation I felt in that moment.

In Jerusalem the Lord procured my salvation through his death on the cross. . . .

In Wiesbaden, he secured my assurance through his written Word of Scripture.

Bless his name.

EPILOGUE

If you have accompanied us all through our journey into assurance, and you still do not have complete certainty that you have been born again . . . you must give serious attention to the fact that perhaps you have not been converted to Christ.

God's plan for your salvation is still this simple: "As many as received Him, to them He gave the right to become children of God, even to those who believe in His name" (John 1:12).